THE FLOWERS OF EVIL

&

ARTIFICIAL PARADISE

THE FLOWERS OF EVIL
&
ARTIFICIAL PARADISE
by
Charles Baudelaire

Published by Solar Books 2008
ISBN 978-0-9799847-7-8
Copyright © Solar Books 2008
All world rights reserved
Les Fleurs du Mal and introduction translated by R.J. Dent
Copyright © R.J. Dent 2008
Artificial Paradise translated by D. Falls
Copyright © D. Falls 2008

Cover illustration:
"Glory and praise to you, Satan"
Odilon Redon, Number 8 of *Les Fleurs du Mal* (1890)
Design:
Tears Corporation

Translator's Acknowledgements:
Moesta et errabunda (Sorrowful and wandering) first appeared in
a revised form in *Acumen Literary Journal* (50th edition).
Metamorphosis of the Vampire first appeared in *Inclement.*
A number of people gave help in a variety of ways. Without them,
this collection would not exist. Thank you to:
Lauren; Barbara Dent; Chris Enright; Gordon Frew; Tony Green;
Audrey Goodhill; Peter & Janet Gooding; Pauline Hawkesford;
Simon Heath; Lionel Pianet; John Philips; Chris Ringrose; Savory
Books; Geoff Smith .

This collection is dedicated to C.B.

CONTENTS

THE FLOWERS OF
EVIL

&

ARTIFICIAL
PARADISE

CHARLES BAUDELAIRE

The buried temple reveals the sewer's dark
sepulchral mouth that dribbles mud and rubies
it is some abominable idol of Anubis
with a muzzle flaming like a savage bark.

Or if the new gas twists the squirming wick
and tries to wipe out every foul rudeness
it haggardly lights an immortal pubis
whose flight needs the streetlamp to stay awake.

Evening – leaves dry outside the city walls
a votive blesses as she sits against
the white marble statue of Baudelaire.
The veil that covers the absent one trembles
as shadow-like she guards the poisoned air
that we breathe in as we asphyxiate.

–Stéphane Mallarmé, "The Tomb Of Baudelaire"

INTRODUCTION

A writer can show no greater courage than to express freedom in the field of morals. From the start, Choderlos de Laclos applied himself to such a task with truly mathematical precision.

1782 is the memorable date of the publication of *Liaisons Dangereuses*, in which Laclos, an artillery officer, tried to apply the laws of triangulation to morality. These laws of triangulation are – as we all know – useful to artillerymen and astronomers.

It is an astonishing contrast! The infinite life which revolves with the firmament obeys the same laws as artillery, which is intended – by the artillerymen – to cause death.

The modern literary spirit was born out of the measured angles so carefully calculated by Laclos. He was the first element discovered by Baudelaire, who was a refined and reasonable explorer from a privileged background, but whose views on modern life contained a particular madness.

Laclos delighted in inspiring the corrupt bubbles that rose from the strange and rich literary mud of the Revolution. Like Diderot, Laclos was the intellectual son of Richardson and Rousseau, and his work was continued by Sade, Restif, Nerciat – some of the most notable philosophical storytellers of the late 18th century. Most of them, in fact, contained the seeds of the modern spirit, and they were poised to create a triumphant new era for arts and letters.

During this nauseating and often brilliant era of Revolution, Baudelaire mingled his spiritualistic poison with the writings of Edgar Allan Poe, a strange American, who had composed, in the poetic field, work which was as disturbing and as marvellous as the work of Laclos.

Baudelaire then is the son of Laclos and Poe. One can easily untangle the influence that each exerted on Baudelaire's prophetic mind and on his work, both so full of originality. As of this year, 1917, when his work enters the public domain, we can not only place him in the front rank of the great French poets, but also award him a place alongside the greatest of universal poets.

The evidence for the influence of the cynical writers of the Revolution on *Les Fleurs du Mal* can be seen everywhere in Baudelaire's correspondence and in his notes. When he decided to translate and adapt Poe's works, strangely, he found a higher lyricism and moral feeling than he had thought was present in the writings of the marvellous Baltimore drunkard and his prohibited readings.

In the novelists of the Revolution, he had discovered the importance of the question of sex.

From the Anglo-Saxons of the same era, such as de Quincey and Poe, Baudelaire had learned that there were artificial paradises. Their methodical exploration – supported by Reason, the revolutionary goddess – enabled him to reach the lyrical heights towards which the mad American predicants had directed Poe, their contemporary. But Reason blinded him, and he abandoned it as soon as he had reached the heights.

Baudelaire then is the son of Laclos and Edgar Allan Poe, but a son who is blind and insane. However, before climbing the peaks, Baudelaire had monitored art and life with admirable precision.

It is also true that he was the first incarnation of the modern mind. It all started with Baudelaire. He gave birth to something which grew, while the naturalists, parnassiens, and symbolists passed by without seeing anything. Meanwhile, although the naturists turned their heads, they did not have the nerve to examine his sublime and monstrous innovations.

For those who are astonished by his questionable birth out of the revolutionary mud and the American pox, the only necessary response is this: Give some consideration to the Bible's explanation of the origin of man from the mud of the earth.

It is true that innovation – initially – had Baudelaire's face. He was the first to blow the minds of modern Europe. But his prophetic brain did not know how to prophesise and Baudelaire did not enter fully into this new spirit. However, it had entered him, and in it he discovered the seeds of a few others that had come before him.

And it would be a fitting punishment if those with great lyrical talent, such as Jean-Jacques Rousseau, were to abandon their art once their lyricism had aged; once their works were repeated by all and sundry; once they were put within easy reach of the vulgar.

However, Baudelaire's works have not properly entered the public domain, and by not being there yet, he can always teach us that an elegant attitude is not at all incompatible with great frankness of expression.

Les Fleurs du Mal is in this respect a document of the first order.

The freedom that prevails in this collection has not prevented it from undoubtedly dominating universal poetry in the late 19th century.

His poetry should no longer be seen as an evil influence.

In his work, Baudelaire rejects the moral side which causes us harm. He does this by forcing us to consider lives and things with a certain pessimistic dilettantism; a dilettantism that we are no longer the dupes of.

Baudelaire looked at the life with a passionate disgust and then set about transforming trees, flowers, women, the entire universe and even art, into something pernicious.

It was madness and not a healthy reality.

However, we should never cease to admire the courage and responsibility of Baudelaire, who did not screen out the contours of life.

Today, it would take the same courage.

Prejudice against the arts has continued to grow, and those who dare speak with as much freedom as Baudelaire did in *Les Fleurs du Mal*, find either the legal authorities against them, or at the very least, the disapproval of their peers and the hypocrisy of the public.

The return to slavery, which one nowadays decorates in the name of freedom, has already resulted in moving letters (particularly those horrified at the decided state of affairs), removing the independent elite, as well as any criticism worthy of the name, until the little freedom that remains today would not dare speak of *Les Fleurs du Mal*.

If he rarely takes part in the modern spirit that he created, we can still use Baudelaire as an example to claim a freedom that gives more to philosophers, to scientists, to artists of all the arts, to restrict it increasingly with regard to letters and to social life.

The social use of literary freedom will become increasingly rare and valuable. The great democracies of the future will not be very liberal for writers; it is wise to plant the flags of poets like Baudelaire very high.

We will be able to wave them from time to time, in order to assemble the small number of still trembling slaves.

–Guillaume Apollinaire (1917)

THE FLOWERS OF EVIL

TO AN IMPECCABLE POET

To a Perfect Magician of French Letters
To My Very Dear and Much Venerated

MASTER AND FRIEND
Théophile Gautier

With the Sentiments
Of the Most Profound Humility
I Dedicate
These Sickly Flowers

C.B.

To the Reader

Folly and error, sin and avarice,
exhaust our bodies, occupy our thoughts,
yet each day we feed our happy remorse,
the same way as beggars nourish their lice.

We sin often, reluctantly confess;
we want our confessions to richly pay,
and when we follow our corrupt pathway,
we use our tears to make our crimes seem less.

On his pillows of evil, Satan lies,
lulling and ensnaring our weak spirits,
then by the subtleties of this chemist,
the metal of our will is vaporized.

We dance on strings held in the devil's hands.
In bad we find the good, then set our trends,
and each day nearer to hell we descend,
moving fearlessly through dark, stinking lands.

As the lecher slobbers gratefully on
the wizened breasts of any ancient whore,
so we steal our pleasures – then demand more,
squeezing the dried fruit till the juice is gone.

Demons take shape inside our drunken dreams,
packed, seething, like a million tapeworms,
and when we breathe in, death fills up our lungs,
a river flowing in us, full of screams.

If all the violence: guns, knives, poison, fire,
and every hateful thing of history,
has not yet ended human destiny,
it's simply that we haven't the desire.

Somewhere among the jackals, panthers, snakes,
the monkeys, scorpions, vultures, and the hounds,
the monsters make their growling, crawling sounds,
and in the evil zoo of our mistakes,

something ugly and evil starts to grow;
it moves slowly, it makes no noise at all,
but it would crush the world into a ball
and gulp it down in one mighty swallow.

Its name is Apathy – the stupid grin,
the tears, the snotty nose it never wipes,
are as well-known as its foul hashish pipe –
it's you, hypocrite reader, brother, twin!

SPLEEN AND THE IDEAL

Benediction

When, at the word of the powers supreme,
a poet appears in this weary world,
his terrified mother starts to blaspheme,
cursing God, who looks pityingly at her:

– "Oh, why, when so many young children die,
did I have to give birth to this foul snake?
And damn that night of lust, of thrills, of sighs,
when I first conceived this most foul mistake!

Since out of every woman you chose me,
to please my gloomy husband, here's my claim:
since I cannot kill this monstrosity,
or drop him right into a furnace flame,

I'll spit my hatred out on him, for he
is a sure sign of heaven's hate; I'll show
you how to raise a twisted, rotten tree,
so no new buds of green will ever grow."

She swallows down the white froth of her hate,
unaware of eternity's designs,
preparing herself for her hellish fate,
where demons worship all maternal crimes.

The child, guarded by an invisible
angel, grows drunk on the warm, golden sun,
the food and wine he eats and drinks till full
is ambrosia, manna from heaven.

He plays outside when clouds bulk and winds rage,
he sings his songs of passion to the cross;
the spirit with him on his pilgrimage
sees he's happy, but feels a sense of loss.

All those he'd love run away, frightened by
his intensity, or tranquillity;
some try to make him suffer, make him cry,
by subjecting him to their cruelty;

a few of them spit into his red wine,
while others flick their ash inside his bread;

some pretend what he's touched has been defiled,
because they fear to go where he has led.

His woman cries out to the busy world:
"He finds me beautiful enough to adore,
so I'll have myself painted in pure gold,
and turn myself into a plated whore.

And then I'll spend my time pleasurably,
bingeing on incense, myrrh, on flesh, on wine,
and when I hear him say he admires me,
I'll laugh, knowing his love's for the divine.

And in the end, I'll grow bored of this farce,
and I'll use my frail, but strong hands to start
stabbing my way, with my long harpy's claws,
straight into the meat of his open heart,

pulling it beating out of his pale breast,
as a young bird will tremble when it's maimed;
to satisfy the hunger of my beasts,
I'll throw it to the ground with great disdain!"

Looking to heaven, seeing a great throne,
the poet raises his arms piously,
and as bright light shines from his lucid soul,
it blocks his view of human cruelty.

– "I praise you, God, for your great gift of pain,
the perfect cure for our impurities,
for when we suffer much, we always gain
the strength to cope with new adversities.

I know that in your heaven, there is a place
you've put aside for me, the poet, so I
can feast with you, and I will sit and face
your power, your virtue, and your throne most high.

To me, suffering is nobility,
untouched by anything of hell or Earth;
when I wear my mystic crown, I will be
the one to tax time and the universe.

Not the lost jewels of ancient Palmyra,
no known metals, no pearls out of the sea,

can be collected by you to make a
beautiful crown of perfect clarity,

because it's made of nothing but pure light
from sacred rays of morning sun that spark
in every human eye, reflecting bright
in mirrors once kept covered in the dark."

The Albatross

Often, for amusement, the sailing crew
catch that bird of the seas, the albatross;
companion on our voyage, it follows
the ship as it slides through the sea's abyss.

When it has been dumped, this once-great sky king,
awkward and ashamed, onto the ship's boards,
it pitifully drags its great white wings
along its feathered sides like useless oars.

This graceful voyager through shades of blue,
once beautiful, is now clumsy and weak;
one sailor mocks the cripple who once flew,
another stubs a pipe out on his beak.

The poet is just like this prince of clouds;
Beyond range, above storms – these are his haunts,
exiled on Earth amidst a jeering crowd,
his giant wings don't permit him to walk.

Elevation

Above the lakes, the valleys, woods, the far-
flung snowy mountain peaks and deepest seas,
beyond the sun, beyond the boundaries
of space and time, beyond the farthest star,

my spirit, you move fast, agile and light;
a swimmer taking pleasure in the sea,
cutting your way through its immensity
with a deliciously virile delight.

Go now! Run from this sickly, morbid place,
find somewhere with a cleaner atmosphere
and drink down gulps of its divine liqueur;
its blazing light that lights its perfect space.

Despite this boring life, this apathy
that weighs down on a constantly numbing
existence, how happy is he whose wings
lift him to fields of great serenity;

the one, whose thought, like skylarks, spread their wings
and find in morning's freedom, perfect flight,
– one who glides through life; knows without effort,
the language of the flowers and all mute things.

Correspondences

Nature's a temple of living columns
that babbles many strange utterances;
this forest of signs, with its covert glances,
watches man as he walks through life alone.

As lasting echoes meet where they resound,
and blend into an obscure unity,
so in the night, with perfect clarity,
all perfumes, colours and sounds correspond.

Some perfumes are as fresh as infant skin,
some have the strength to grow and to expand,
some are as smooth as oboe music, green

as new grass, or are rich and triumphant,
such as amber, musk, benjamin, incense,
whose songs sing rapture to spirit and sense.

'I love the memory...'

I love the memory of those naked days,
when the sun gilded statues with its rays;

when men and women loved agility;
no shame was caused by sensuality,
as heaven lovingly caressed their skin,
they watched the health of their fleshy machines.
Nature, then rich, generous and kind,
carefully nourished her offspring – mankind,
and like a loving she-wolf she would nurse
at her brown teats the entire universe.
Man, elegant, robust and strong, was proud
of the beauties who claimed he should be crowned,
pure virgin girls, the fresh untainted fruit,
whose smooth and firm flesh invites every bite!

When the poet tries to imagine now
those naked joys, in places that allow
man and woman to be naked, a cold
and gloomy feeling envelopes his soul.
He sees a black, terrifying tableau:
monstrosities crying out for their clothes;
twisted bodies, fat uglies needing masks,
the crooked, wasted, flabby, the grotesque –
who some practical god, serene and calm,
forced into metal clothes when they were born,
and every one as pale as candle wax,
who gnaw at their debauchery and sex
who drag with them their parents' stupid vice
of bringing hideous progeny to life.

It's true we have, in our corrupted world,
beauties not known to the people of old:
we have the results of the languorous arts,
and faces gnawed away by cancerous hearts,
but these inventions of our tardy muse
will never let the sickest ones refuse
to give a tribute to eternal youth,
– to sacred youth, with its clear, simple views,
its clear-eyed gaze, fresh as a waterfall
that pours down constantly over us all;
as carefree as the flowers, the birds, the sky;
the perfumes, warmth and songs that never die.

Beacons

Rubens:
Garden of sleep, river of forgetting,
pillow of flesh, unloved in chastity,
whose life flows onwards, never abating,
as air in sky, or water in the sea.

Leonardo:
Shadowy mirror most profound, in which,
charming angels, with soft, mysterious smiles,
loom in the shadows of the glaciers
and pines bordering lands that stretch for miles.

Rembrandt:
Hospital full of sorrowful murmurs,
and decorated with only one cross;
a filthy place, full of sad, tearful prayers,
where winter cold slowly freezes the lost.

Michelangelo:
Vague place where one sees Hercules and Christ
together. In twilight, phantoms linger –
and rising straight up from below, they try
to shred their shrouds and reach out cold fingers.

Puget:
Melancholy emperor of convicts,
a boxer's fury, a faun's impudence,
always finding pale beauty in the sick;
a proud heart, weak, enfeebled with jaundice.

Watteau:
A carnival at which all good, kind hearts
are butterflies, errant and flamboyant;
in cool scenery, beneath shining lights,
their madness drives them in their whirling dance.

Goya:
A host of unknown things in black nightmares,
at witches' sabbats; a roasting foetus,
old women at their mirrors like young girls,
adjusting their stockings to tempt demons.

Delacroix:
In the deep shadow of the new green firs,
the evil angels haunt a lake of blood,
while strange, soft fanfares, written by Weber,
echo to poisoned skies above the woods.

These maledictions, blasphemies, laments,
these ecstasies, these tears, these cries, these shouts,
echo throughout a thousand labyrinths;
it is the opium for mortal hearts!

It's the cry of a thousand sentinels,
an order shouted through a megaphone;
one beacon on a thousand citadels,
and in the woods it's hunters blowing horns.

This, oh Lord, is the best witness we have
which will let the world see our dignity;
those ardent sobs that roll from age to age
have come to die on your eternity!

The Sick Muse

My poor muse, how are you doing today?
Your hollow eyes are full of night's grim hold,
and now I see that your complexion's grey
with madness and horror, silent and cold.

Did the green succubus and the red imp
pour out their fear and love from their foul urn?
Did nightmare, with its deadly tyrant's grip
pull you down to the city they would burn?

Let your Christian blood flow in rhythmic waves –
I want you to be healthy, fit and strong,
to think the great thoughts of a thinking man,

and hear the sounds of ancient verse and plays,
reigning in turn over our father's songs,
and the lord of the harvest, the god Pan.

The Venal Muse

Lover of palaces, muse of my heart,
will you, when January's brings cold blights,
have enough embers to warm your feet,
during the blackness of snow-covered nights?

Will you be able to warm your cold flesh
with the nocturnal rays that shine on you,
and when your mouth is as dry your purse,
will you harvest gold rain from vaults of blue?

To earn your evening bread, you may have to
swing a censer like a bored choirboy;
chant to a god you don't believe exists,

or, like a starving acrobat, do tricks
as you smile through your tears, and try hard to
entertain those who'd like to pass you by.

The Wicked Monk

On the walls of the ancient cloister
are great paintings to holy verity,
whose display thaws the innards of the pious,
and the coldness of their austerity.

Back then, when Christ's message was still quite new,
more than one monk, long gone from memory,
took the cemetery as his studio,
and portrayed death with great simplicity.

– My soul's a tomb I'm in eternally,
and I, wicked cenobite, must stay in
my cell, no decorations, no pictures.

O idle monk! when shall I ever learn
to change my misery into the work
of my hands and the love of all I see?

The Enemy

My youth was full of storms, all quite savage,
but sometimes cut across by brilliant suns;
the thunderstorms and rains have so ravaged
my garden that just hardy fruits remain.

The autumn of ideas is all I touch,
as I carefully use my rake and spade
to collect and renew the flooded earth,
from holes as big and deep as any grave.

And what if these new flowers I dream don't find
the mystical food they need to grow straight
in this washed-out earth, this soil of sand?

– O sorrow! Life eats time – it always could;
an obscure enemy chews on our heart,
increasing its strength as it drinks our blood.

Bad Luck

As time is short and Art is long,
to carry such a heavy weight
one needs a tough and eager heart,
and to be like Sisyphus – strong.

Far from celebrity's great tombs,
towards a lonely cemetery,
my heart beats its way to my grave,
tapping like some funeral drum.

– Many a gem lies buried deep,
far away from the probes and spades,
forgotten in the dark, asleep;

many a flower spills with regret
its soft perfume like a secret
in the profoundest solitude.

A Previous Life

I once lived under giant porticoes
that the sea's suns tinged with a thousand fires,
and whose straight and majestic great pillars
resembled, at evening, basalt grottoes.

The heavy seas beneath the rolling skies;
the constant music and its harmonies,
merged in a solemn and mystical way,
reflecting sunset colours in my eyes.

And in the centre of the sky and waves
I lived a life of voluptuous ease,
for I had perfumed, scented, naked slaves,

who fanned me every day with huge palm leaves;
whose only job was to stay and take care
of the secret sorrow that kept me there.

Travelling Gypsies

The tribe of prophets with wild, ardent eyes
took to the road yesterday, their young ones
on their backs, appeasing their fierce hungers
with treasure from full breasts hanging nearby.

The men, with shining weapons, lithely stride
beside the vehicles their families hide in;
with heavy eyes and with a deep yearning,
they search for absent dreams in the grey sky.

The cricket, inside his sandy domain,
regards them as they pass, doubles his song;
nature, who loves them, increases her green,

brings water from rocks, makes flowers bloom in sand;
a sign these travellers well understand –
their dark future is a familiar land.

Man and the Sea

Free man, you will always cherish the sea!
It's your mirror – you contemplate your soul
constantly in its swell as it unrolls;
your spirit's gulf deepens as bitterly.

You love to plunge into your own image,
to kiss your eyes and heart, and then something
will distract you from the song it should sing –
those loud lamentations that sound savage.

Both of you have your secrets in the dark:
man, none yet know the depths of your abyss;
sea, none have known your intimate riches
or the secrets you so jealously guard!

And yet throughout innumerable years,
you've battled on without remorse or rage,
because you both admire death and carnage,
eternal enemies, fighting brothers.

Don Juan in Hell

When Don Juan descends to the underground,
he hands his ferry fare to old Charon,
a beggar with eyes that are fierce and proud,
whose grip on each oar is vengeful and strong.

Sad women writhe beneath the blackened sky,
showing their pendulous breasts through open holes
in their gowns. And like cattle set to die,
they follow him, uttering sad, low moans.

Sganarelle smiles, demanding cash right there,
while, with a trembling hand, old Don Luis
shows to the dead who stand on the near shore,
the audacious son who mocks his white hair.

Elvira, thin, chaste, shivering with grief,

stands by her former lover – her false spouse,
and seems to ask for one last smile from him,
warm with the tenderness of his first vow.

Standing in armour, a great man of stone
steers the boat through the water with great skill,
but leaning on his sword, the calm hero,
regards the wake and sees nothing at all.

Punishment for Pride

In those far off times when theology
flourished with power and endless energy,
one story tells of a doctor of arts
–after he had cured a few uncaring hearts
by stirring them from their dark lethargy,
and lifting himself towards celestial glory,
to where only pure spirits could be found,
and using methods he had doubts about–
who, afraid that he might have climbed too high,
still shouted out, in full Satanic pride:
"Little Jesus, I've praised you to the skies!
But, if I'd chosen instead to deride
your glory, you'd be dragged through shamefulness;
be no more than a pathetic foetus!"

Immediately all of his reason failed;
this sun's brilliance was abruptly veiled
as chaos poured into intelligence;
a living temple, full of opulence,
with walls that had sheltered an intellect,
now full of darkness, constantly silent;
a gloomy cellar with a missing key.
From then, like some beast in captivity,
no longer knowing anything, he crossed
summer and winter fields, confused and lost,
dirty, useless, a worn-out thing, beaten,
and often the sport of spiteful children.

Beauty

Mortals, I'm a dream of stone, beautiful.
My breast, upon which everyone is bruised,
inspires in the poet a love that's huge
and more solid than matter – eternal.

A silent sphinx enthroned on a vast cloud,
my heart is snow, whiter than any swan;
I hate movement that ruins perfect lines;
I'm never sad and never laugh out loud.

The poets, seeing the majestic stances
I've stolen from the most perfect statues,
fill their days with work; their ardent glances

are into mirrors that reflect beauty
in everything; to ensnare them I use
my eyes with their eternal clarity.

The Ideal

None of those beauties found in photographs;
the spoiled items of our degraded days,
with laced boots, glossed nails, eyes half-
closed, can satisfy a longing like mine.

No matter how a cameraman poses
his troupe of anaemic beauties, I feel
nothing because, among those pale roses,
I cannot find the one – my red ideal.

The need that's deep within my heart's abyss,
is you, Lady Macbeth, your soul of crimes;
those dreams born in the storm by Aeschylus,

or you, night child of Michelangelo,
your charms shaped for the mouths of the Titans,
who'll twist you into every bizarre pose.

A Giantess

If Nature used her power to fill the place
with monstrous infants, never before seen,
I would live close to a young giantess,
like a cat at the feet of a young queen.

I'd watch her body and soul slowly flower
and grow strong with each terrifying game;
I'd wonder if her heart was touched by fire
but hidden by the soft mists in her eyes;

I'd travel over her gigantic form;
Take time to explore her enormity,
and then in summer, when the pale sun,

impelled her to rest stretching across fields,
I'd sleep in the shade of one of her breasts,
– a peaceful town at the foot of a hill.

Jewels

Knowing my needs, my dearest one was nude,
only wearing her jewellery for me,
these items made her seem perfectly lewd;
a slave in a harem eager to please.

As she moved slowly, gems danced, ringing out
subtle music – a mix of light and tone,
and I was transfixed by her jewelled pout,
lit up by sparkling metals and rare stones.

Reaching the bed, she spread voluptuously,
letting me love her in the ways she pleased,
my lust, like an ocean, was full and deep,
rising to her – a cliff mounted by seas.

Her eyes fixed on me, like a tiger tamed,
dreamily she tried various poses,
her candour and her willingness combined
to give charm to each metamorphosis.

Her arms and her legs, her loins and her thighs,
oil-polished, undulating like a swan,
were like a feast before my starving eyes,
then belly, breasts, her clusters on my vine.

When she thrust forward, this fallen angel
troubled me greatly, fuelling my desire,
until my lustful soul was half-deranged;
a cold crystal thrown on a raging fire.

In her I could discern a new design
of woman; smooth torso and rounded hips;
her perfect height setting off perfect lines;
her tawny skin deserving of worship.

And as the candle-light prepared to die,
and its low flames gently lit the chamber,
each time there sounded a contented sigh,
our warm flesh blushed the colour of amber.

The Mask

An allegorical statue in the style of the Renaissance

For Ernest Christophe, sculptor.

Let's look at this Grace, made by Florentines;
the smooth undulations of her body
have elegance and force subtly combined.
This woman, a truly marvellous piece,
so slender and so strong, should now be placed
inside a penthouse suite, furnished in style,
for the constant enjoyment of some prince.

– Also, notice the provocative smile,
containing ecstasy and arrogance;
over the fine features, a veil's been placed,
half-covering a mocking and sly glance;
a look that looks as though it wants to say:
"I wear pleasure as clothes, love as a crown."
This is a work of stunning majesty;
its sensual charms have powers to arouse –
let's look around the back of this beauty…

Yes, it's a shock! – as though art has blasphemed!
This perfect woman, her body divine,
is suddenly a monster with two heads!

– No! it's just a mask, a clever design;
a mask of anguish, showing a grimace.
Look underneath this mask's atrocities
and you'll see the real head, the sincere face
that's mirrored by this other face that lies.
I feel so sorry for this poor beauty;
tears stream down her face, straight into my heart,
and there's something about her falsity
that makes me drunk on every tear she spurts.

– But why does she cry, this perfect beauty?
She could have the world at her feet – conquered.
Something troubles her – some great mystery.

She's unhappy because she's truly lived!
It's life that hurts her! Life causes her pain!
Her sadness comes from knowing tomorrow,
will be the same – she'll live her day again,
then one more... then one more... As we all do.

Hymn to Beauty

Beauty, are you from heaven; are you from
the abyss? Your glance, hellish and divine,
looks without judgement at goodness and crime;
you have the same effect as a good wine.

In your eyes are the sunset and the dawn;
you scatter perfumes like an evening storm;
your kiss is a potion from a sealed jar
that makes heroes afraid and children warm.

Are you from the black gulf or from the stars?
Fate, like a trained dog, follows you along
as you sow seeds of joy and disaster;
you rule the world and answer to no one.

Beauty, you walk over the dead, mocking;
of your jewels, horror is not the most cruel,

murder is the one that's the most shocking,
dancing in your navel, a loving jewel.

Candle, the mayfly flies into your fire,
then crackles, flares, dies, saying: "Lovely flame."
The lover loving his love with desire,
looks like a dying man stroking his tomb.

Who cares where you are from? What's important,
monstrous Beauty – ingenious, frightening,
is that your eyes or smiles open portals
to kinds of love that I have never known?

Angel or Siren? – what you are does not
matter – as long as with your velvet eyes,
and with perfume, with rhythm, and with light,
you make the world better, you make time fly.

Exotic Perfume

Eyes shut on a warm evening in autumn,
I breathe in the scent of your warm breasts – and
see the gold coast of an inviting land
made bright and warm by the heat of the sun;

An idle island where nature supplies
delicious fruits that hang from perfect trees;
men who have slim and vigorous physiques;
beautiful women with large, candid eyes.

Your fragrance leads me to this charming place;
I see a port crowded with masts and sails,
all battered by the sea storms they have faced.

The scent of green tamarind is dancing
in circles in the air, whispy and frail,
and mixing with the fishermen's chanting.

Hair

Fleece, dark curls, rolling in waves down your bare
neck; perfumed locks full of strong fragrances.
Tonight, when I breath in your mane of hair,
I'll be transported to a land somewhere,
your perfect tresses blowing in the breeze.

A distant, vanished, almost absent world;
African rhythms, Oriental charms
are there in the wild forest of your curls;
your music on which anyone can sail,
as I now drift along on your perfume.

I'll go to where the sap-filled men and trees,
rest from the ardent heat in burning lands;
strong tresses, be waves that take me away.
You are a dream, a vast ebony sea,
of boats, of sails, of sea, of sun, of sand:

a noisy, busy port where I may drink
great waves of colour and of sound and scent;
where ships, bringing their gold and watered silk,
open their arms to embrace the vast brink
of a pure sky trembling with eternal heat.

Into this black sea where other seas swell,
I'll dip my lovingly rapturous head
and then, caressed by rolling waves, I will
find you again, idleness that's fertile
enough to lull me into a sweet bed.

Blue hair, pavilion of night's darkness,
an immense and rounded sky splashed full of stars;
in the softness of your untwisted locks,
I breathe in the intoxicating scents
of oil, of coconut, of musk, of tar.

Forever, in your heavy mane, my hand
will scatter sapphires and pearls and rubies,
to make sure my desire for you is heard.
You're the oasis where I dream my words;
the wine glass from which I drink memories.

'I adore you as I adore the night…'

I adore you as I adore the night,
yet you seem so sad, beautiful, silent.
The more you elude me, the more I love
you, ornament of my night, there above,
you fill ironic space, separate me
from the immensity of the blue sky.

I writhe beneath your body like a worm,
feeding upon your perfect, corpse-like form,
and cherish you, though you are harsh and cruel –
a coldness that I find so beautiful.

'You'd sleep with everybody in the world…'

You'll sleep with everybody in the world,
you foul whore! Boredom makes you cruel enough
to exercise your teeth in perverse games;
you need to chew on new hearts every day.
Your eyes, alight like windows late at night,
or yew trees strung with lanterns for a fête,
bore insolently into the self-conscious,
but never know quite what their beauty is.

Unfeeling sex-machine, perversity
makes you a profit. You suck the world dry
and feel pride – you look at your reflection
in your mirrors, at your pale attractions –
for they contain the seeds of all you've done.
Is it then that you're ashamed of what's to come?
– of nature fooling you with secret plans;
of you, woman, queen of the lecherous,
giving unwilling birth to genius –

a vile child, who'll grow into a great man.

Still not Satisfied

Bizarre deity, as brown as the night,
with your perfumes of musk and Havana,
some obi's trick, Faust of the savannah,
ebony sorceress, child of midnight,

the fragrant taste of your sweet soft lips thrills
me more than wine, opium, anything;
my desire moves to you in caravan –
a reservoir from which I drink my fill.

Your two dark eyes are flaming; just for kicks,
you burn my body with pitiless flames;
I try, but nine times is just for the Styx,

and afterwards, I never find the will
to drive you away, or to break your heart
in bed by becoming your Queen of Hell.

'When she walks, it's as though she dances...'

When she walks, it's as though she dances,
for in her sequinned clothes she undulates
the same way as a snake sways to the strange,
thin music that pours from a fakir's flute.

But like the empty desert skies and sands,
she feels nothing for human suffering,
and like the waves that break on distant lands,
for those she has broken, she feels nothing.

Her eyes are hardened stone, gems of onyx;
her strange, symbolic nature is a mix
of purest angel and of antique sphinx.

Dressed in her diamonds and gold and steel,
she shines brightly like distant nebulae,
but without any real heat – quite sterile.

Snake Dance

I love to look at your body,
　　　　it's beautiful, indolent one;
there is a shimmering quality
　　　　to the silken gleam of your skin.

and in the depths of your long hair
　　　　with its rich scents and its perfumes;
a scented and a wayward sea
　　　　of waves of brown and green and blue,

my soul, like a ship that is stirred
　　　　by the first sea winds of the day,
dreamily starts its voyage for
　　　　another sky that's far away.

Your eyes, in which nothing that's kind
　　　　or bitter can ever be told,
are two frozen jewels, mingling
　　　　their iron centres with their gold.

Seeing you walk so musically,
　　　　so beautifully that you entrance,
it's easy to be reminded
　　　　of every sensuous snake dance.

As you grow sleepy – it is late,
　　　　your childish head grows indolent
and heavy with the graceful weight
　　　　of every new-born elephant.

Your body sways and stretches like
　　　　the finest ship money can buy,
swaying from side to side, plunging
　　　　its masts and sails into the sea.

Like streams swollen by melting ice
　　　　from groaning polar glaciers,
up to the edge of your sharp teeth,
　　　　your sweet mouth's water rises.

I think I drink Bohemian wine,
           it's bitter, powerful and tart;
a liquid night sky that scatters
           a million stars upon my heart.

A Carcass

Remember that thing that we saw, my love,
           on a beautiful, fresh morning in June:
a disgusting carcass by a path's curve,
           in a new flowerbed scattered with stones,

legs in the air, like a lusting woman,
           burning, sweating with a mass of poisons,
nonchalantly and shamelessly showing
           its bloated stomach full of noxious fumes.

The sun shone down upon this rottenness,
           as to roast it with its golden fire,
so giving back a hundredfold at least
           all that was joined together by nature;

until it burst apart, an opening flower
           watched by the heavens, a superb carcass
with an overwhelming stink; you were sure
           you'd faint right there and then upon the grass.

The flies were buzzing on flesh quite putrid,
           and out of which poured black battalions
of maggots, flowing like a thick liquid
           along the length of those living tatters.

The whole thing rose and fell in liquid waves
           rushing, seething, sparkling, heaving, moving,
swollen with breath, as if the cadaver,
           was somehow alive and multiplying.

And this world gave out strange musical sounds,
           like flowing water or the blowing breeze,
or grain that harvesters rhythmically pound,
           then shake and turn in their baskets with ease.

Deformed, it faded as fragmented dreams;
        a sketchbook full of forgotten outlines
and which the artist has to then complete
        with no help, but from memory alone.

From back behind the rocks, a restless bitch
        watched us with fierce eyes, as it angrily
waited for that one moment it could snatch
        the piece of bone she had almost pulled free.

– And you will be just like this rottenness,
        the same as this horrible infection,
you, star of my eyes, sun of my nature,
        you, my perfect angel and my passion.

Yes, you will be like this, my graceful queen,
        right after the last rites have been intoned,
when you go, beneath grass and flowering weeds,
        to moulder alone there amongst the bones.

and then, my love, make sure you tell the worms,
        the ones who now devour you with soft mouths,
that I kept the essence, the divine form
        of what I'd call my decomposing love.

From the Depths I Cry Out

Please pity me – yes you, the one I love:
my heart is buried in this dark abyss;
there's no horizon in this universe,
where horrors float through the darkness above;

A cold sun hangs above for half the year,
and for the other half, night covers all;
a country more empty than the Earth's poles;
– no animals, no trees, no rivers here.

No horror in the world could now surpass
the cold cruelty of this sun of ice,
or the immensity of night's chaos;

I envy the fate of the vilest beast,

that plunges into its sleep, stupefied,
so slowly does time's skein take to unwind.

The Vampire

Like a knife thrust, you stabbed right in
to the centre of my sad heart;
and you, with the power of demons,
came to me to tear me apart,

by making my spirit bow down,
in your bed and in your domain;
I hate you though to you I'm bound,
just like a convict to his chains;

just like the gambler to the game;
just like the drunk to the whiskey;
just like vermin to carrion,
– damn you to hell, damned you will be.

I prayed for a huge battle blade,
so I could fight for freedom; but
I asked for poison to be made,
in case my terror needed it.

Poison and sword both turned away
and in disgust, they said to me:
"You are not worthy to be free
from your accursed slavery.

You fool! – if only our efforts
could mean that somehow you'd been saved,
but your kiss would resuscitate
your vampire's body in its grave."

Lethe

Crouch on my heart, tigress that I adore,
you cruel and silent, indolent mistress;
I long to plunge my fingers in the depths
of your thick, perfumed, long and heavy hair.

I'll bury my head, when it is aching,
in your underclothes, inhale your perfume
and breathe in, like a flower's fading bloom,
the sweet aroma of our lovemaking.

I long to sleep a sleep as sweet as death!
I'll now be content to be nobody,
for over your beautifully bronzed body,
I've kissed my endless kisses, breathed my breath.

The perfection of you in your vast bed
swallows my agony, eases my pain;
your mouth makes me forget myself, my name,
your kisses fire my body, whirl my head.

My destiny with you is my delight;
you can command me; I have no real choice;
to be your martyr is one of my joys,
simply because you set my soul alight.

Now I've found a kind of tranquillity,
as I softly suck between my warm lips
the delightfully hardening brown tips
of perfect breasts that will never love me.

'After a night spent with a Jewish whore...'

After a night spent with a Jewish whore,
as we lay sprawled like corpses side by side,
I dreamt, not of the girl for whom I'd paid,
but of the lovely woman I adored.

I thought of her beauty, her majesty,
her candid gaze, her strength, her sinuous grace,

42

her hair, hanging perfumed around her face;
I grew aroused at this sweet memory…

How I desire your body here to kiss
from your feet and right up to your dark hair;
to unearth the deep treasures of your flesh.

Perhaps, some evening, there will be one tear
that forms in the corner of your cold eyes,
melting your cruel reign, you queen of ice.

Posthumous Remorse

Sullen beauty, when you sleep in your tomb
beneath a black headstone, all you will have
to lie in is a damp vault or deep grave;
this will be your retreat, your stately home.

When that black stone presses on your scared breast,
and on your thighs, at which desire once drank,
and stops your heart from beating out its thanks,
and makes your agile feet pause for a rest;

and when the grave – which understands yearning
(all poets and graves have similar thoughts),
asks you, on nights you're restlessly turning:

"What is it you think you have you gained, you whore,
by not knowing why all the dead cry out!"
– it's then the worms find you and start to gnaw.

The Cat

Come, my fine cat, onto my loving heart,
      pull in your claws, relax,
let me plunge into your beautiful eyes;
      metal and agate mixed.

When my fingertips caress at leisure
      your spine's elastic curves,

and my hand grows drunk with pleasure
          on your electric nerves,

I think about my woman – how much like
          you she is, dear beast,
her look as deep as wounds, sharp as a spike,

          and, head to toe, a scent,
a thrilling perfume that emanates from
          her body, lithe and brown.

The Duel

Two warriors are fighting – their weapons
are blood-splattered and glisten all over;
their contest, their clash of steel started from
youth's fight of honour over a lover.

We've lost our youth – with teeth and nails we maim
each other, love; when these two realize
their swords have lost their edge, they'll do the same;
their fighting hearts won't want to compromise.

Their struggles roll them into a ravine,
to which leopards and wild cats slink to view
the fighters, as their flesh is ripped by thorns.

– This grim ravine, so full of friends we know,
must be the best place for us all to stay,
until our human hatred fades away.

The Balcony

Mother of memories, mistress of mistresses,
to you I owe my duties, my pleasures!
Do you recall beautiful caresses,
tender moments and evenings of leisure?
– Mother of memories, mistress of mistresses.

The evenings lit by a soft candle glow;
sunsets on the balcony; rose-tinged mist;
we spoke of our future, we whispered low.
How sweet your soul, how beautiful your breasts.
Those evenings lit by a soft candle glow.

How warm the sun was on lovely evenings,
how deep the sky! And how my heart pounded
as I leaned against you, my adored queen,
and breathed in the rich perfume of your blood.
How warm the sun was on lovely evenings.

The night surrounded us like a high wall,
and in the dusk, my eyes looked into yours,
and I drank in your breath; sweetest of all,
I softly touched your feet – that touch endures.
The night surrounded us like a high wall.

I know how to recreate happiness,
relive my past, resting against your thighs.
Now I can search for beauty nowhere else,
but in your heart, your body's symmetries,
I know how to recreate happiness!

Those promises, those kisses, those perfumes,
will they spring up from places we can't see,
just as the new sun climbs into the blue,
after being purified in the seas?
– These promises! These kisses! These perfumes!

The Possessed

The sun is out. Its pale copy, the moon,
is covered in shadows. So are my days.
You sleep or smoke; you're silent or sullen,
often apathetic – they're just your ways.

I love you the same way an eclipsed star
emerges from its cloud screen – throws out light.
When you're volatile, you seek out danger,
your rose tattoo revealed, your clothes too tight.

45

You make your eyes shine by looking at lights,
moisten your lips, pout, provoke and tease louts;
so be yourself - you're pleasure's my delight.

Be night, be day, be dusk, dawn, false or true;
every nerve in my taut body cries out:
- *My beloved demon, I adore you!*

A Phantom

1 - Darkness

Sentenced by fate and sent by destiny
into a deep cave of endless sadness,
so dark no light can penetrate its depths,
and at night, alone and solitary,

I'm condemned by a mocking god to paint
the shadowed darkness that surrounds me there;
to be a funeral chef and prepare
and carefully roast and eat my own heart.

Sometimes, a faint shape forms and shines and grows;
a gently graceful and wonderful phantom
that stretches sinuously, in ways I know...

It's then I recognise my visitor;
a black, luminous, exotic being -
I'd recognise her beauty anywhere.

2 - Perfume

Reader, have you sometimes sniffed the incense
they use in cathedrals, or have you breathed
in the smell of musk, or vanilla leaves,
or any other strong, powerful scent

that contains such magic, such charm and power,
it makes the past come alive? This is how
lovers, who, with their loved one, all know
to only pick memory's perfect flowers...

In the depths of her tangled, heavy hair,
I smell the scent of incense, of our bed;
the hastily-strewn clothes, the underwear,

all give off aromas that whirl the head –
the scent of a savage, interlocked pair;
that strong perfume which always smells like fur.

3 – The Frame

Just as a frame adds to the work of art
–no matter how talented the artist–
and something strange and enchanting
reveals its nature, setting it apart,

so do silks, mirrors, metals, jewellery,
fit around the rare beauty of this one;
nothing obscures her sheer perfection,
and every item frames her perfectly.

It's almost as though one day she'll confess
that everyone has begged her for her love;
she likes to have her sensual nakedness

kissed by soft velvets, satins, silks and lace,
and laze, but when she occasionally moves,
it's with a simian and child-like grace.

4 – The Portrait

Our fiery passions have burnt out.
Sickness and death have done away
with everything: your gentle eyes;
your mouth, in which I drowned my heart;

your endless, passionate kisses,
made me more virile than sunlight.
And what's left now? Ashes and dust;
a fading sketch of three roses,

just left, like me, alone, to die,
pushed by Time – a nasty old man
who rubs his hands greedily…

Time kills all life and kills all art,
but time can't kill the memory
of her – my pleasure and delight.

'I give you these verses...'

I give you these verses so that my name
can travel forward into future times,
when humans dream their dreams with awake minds;
a ship loaded with a cargo of fame.

Your legacy, confused in troubled times,
disturbs readers, like music's microtones;
the power of the work that you have done
is clear and strong and here in my proud rhymes.

An outcast – unwanted by the highest
and lowest, you came and went; a shadow
that only I noticed. And you have left

your mark. You trod softly; serenely gazed
on stupid mortals presuming to know
your jet eyes – angel with a golden face.

Always the Same

"Tell me, where does your strange sadness come from?
It's like a wave breaking over a black rock."
My answer's this: I hurt from the world's pain,
my heart's been harvested – I suffer lack;

it's suffering, that's all – no mystery,
too dark to look at, just as you're too bright,
so no more questions, curious beauty.
I love your gentle voice, but please be quiet.

Don't ask again. Use your delightful breath
for laughter instead – find pleasure in life,
because we are all subtly tied to death.

Tell me stories to make me drunk, tell lies,
sing me beautiful songs, then let me dive
into a dreaming sleep deep in your eyes.

Entirely

A demon came to my high room
to see me early this morning;
trying to trick me to my doom,
it said:"I was just wondering,

if you could tell me, please, which parts
of your woman's lithe nakedness
delight you the most; would you start
with her thighs? Or is it her breasts

which taste the sweetest?" – I answered
that triple-damned malignant thing,
saying:"I personally prefer
all parts of her – yes, everything.

Her whole body gives me delight.
I ignore nothing; to choose one
is to lose out. She's dark like night
and yet she dazzles like the dawn.

Her body has a harmony
that's perfect, far beyond the words;
of anyone who tried to see
each single note of every chord.

It's metamorphosis – a trick;
she makes my senses grow confused;
her breath makes beautiful music,
her voice makes delightful perfume!"

'What will you say tonight…'

What will you say tonight, poor lonely soul?
What will you say tonight, withered up heart,
to someone so good and so beautiful,
whose divine beauty makes your life restart?

– With pride we'll sing her praises and her name;
there's nobody as tender as she is;
her skin is scented like angel's perfume
and the light in her eyes makes us believe.

Sometimes, in the night's silent solitude,
or in the street among the seething crowd,
her presence dances like a living flame,

saying: "I'm Beauty, and I command this –
you love me above every goddess;
I'm an angel with every woman's name."

The Living Torch

In front of me, they float like eyes of light;
a cosmic trick or something magnetized,
leading me on, bright brothers in the night;
I follow them, eagerness in my eyes.

They guide me away from the open graves,
lead me to many beautiful new ways;
they guide me well, but somehow I'm their slave;
they are a living torch I must obey.

Mysterious eyes, you burn so strangely bright;
like scented candles burning through the day,
the sun cannot put out your perfect light.

You look like brand new life – you push death back
with your brightness, as you lead me away
to stars no sun can ever fade to black.

To One Who is Too Happy

Your look, your pose, your inner grace,
are prettier than a picture;
as a breeze blows across a moor,
so laughter plays across your face.

The glum one that you brush against
stops, dazzled by your body heat,
from which constantly emanates
your sensual power, erotic lust.

The multi-coloured clothes you wear;
your bright, new-age gypsy outfit,
brings to the mind of the poet
a rioting ballet of flowers.

You dress your colourful spirit
in your lithe body, rainbow child.
Your mad behaviour drives me wild;
I love you, but sometimes I hate.

When it's too much, I find some rest
in a nearby garden I like,
and there as I negate my spite,
I feel the sun tear through my chest,

until I feel my common sense
overcome by the garden's power;
it's then I crush a tiny flower,
to punish nature's insolence.

But what I'd really like is to
explore all your body's treasures
and so learn of each new pleasure
you hold for me, it holds for you.

And then I'd punish you. I'd pin
you down and squeeze your breasts, beat you
until you were red, sore and bruised.
Then I'd cut a slit in your skin,

and sister, here's what else I'd do;
in a moment of strong passion,
in between those lips I'd fashioned,
I'd squirt my venom into you.

Reversibility

Angel of happiness, do you know grief,
or shame, sadness, apathy, or remorse,
or the terrors of nights without relief,
that crush the heart into a paper ball?
Angel of happiness, do you know grief?

Angel of goodness, do you know the hate;
hands clenched in shadow and the bitter tears,
revenge pounding through veins; a loud drum beat,
leading us on to act against our fears?
Angel of goodness, do you know the hate?

Angel of health, do you know diseases;
eroded lives inside the hospitals,
life's exiles, victims of strokes and seizures,
squinting at sunlight, all wards overfull?
Angel of health, do you know diseases?

Angel of beauty, do you know aging;
the fear of lines, decrepitude, decay,
the pain of seeing a loved one gauging
one's visible collapse day upon day?
Angel of beauty, do you know aging?

Angel of joy, of lights, of ecstasy,
a dying man would fully recover
in the perfumes of your perfect body;
all I ask of you, Angel, is your prayers,
Angel of joy, of lights, of ecstasy.

Confession

Sweet and lovely creature, that single time
        we briefly touched electrified
my whole body – now I find I daydream
        of you – the memory won't fade.

It was late and just like a new-made coin,
        the harvest moon shone down brightly,
it's broad beams like small silver streams pouring
        over the dark, sleeping city.

Along house-fronts, past doors and alleyways,
        cats slinked on past us furtively,
their ears cocked, then, like loving shadows, they
        gave us their night time company.

Suddenly, at the most crucial moment
        of our intimacy that night,
you changed – from a delicate instrument,
        trembling with sensual delight,

to someone who cried out as though in pain.
        Your cries ripped the thin air apart;
cries I don't want to have to hear again,
        echoing through the streets and night.

It was the sound of a dying innocence;
        the sound of a child, locked away;
one who is a family embarrassment
        and not let out during the day.

That sound said many things to me. It said:
        "Things aren't always as they might seem,
because behind the mask, though in disguise,
        selfishness can always be seen.

It's tough work having to be beautiful;
        I wear my ready-to-wear face;
I'm like a dancer who has a slight fall
        and yet keeps her fake smile in place.

It's stupid to trust anybody's heart.
      Those two huge lies – love and beauty,
end up forgotten, trampled, torn apart,
      swept away by eternity."

Now, I think of that night; our touch, the moon,
      and your cry in the night's silence,
and then that horrible secret, not spoken
      aloud, but what your heart confessed.

Spiritual Dawn

A strange metamorphosis takes place when
the rose and white dawn light shines on the beds
of the promiscuous. In tired heads,
an angel of perfection awakens

and spiritual skies of a perfect blue
are then open to these earthbound dreamers –
but they are pulled to earth by their choices.
Dearest angel, here's how I think of you;

after all the one-night stands; the orgies,
a memory of you – your pink dawn charm,
appears before my avaricious eyes.

As candle-flames are outshone by the sun,
so you, my immortal and brightest star,
shine on humanity – again, you've won.

Evening Harmony

Now it is time: vibrating on its stem,
each flower gives off an aromatic scent;
sounds and perfumes mingle in evening light;
the sad, slow waltz begins to play again.

Each flower gives off an aromatic scent;
violins play the notes that cause most pain;

the sad, slow waltz begins to play again,
the clouds in the sky rumble, turbulent.

Violins play the notes that cause most pain;
sensitive hearts, avoid the void you hate;
the clouds in the sky rumble, turbulent;
the sun is drowned in human blood again.

Sensitive hearts, avoid the void you hate;
recall the past as often as you can;
the sun is drowned in human blood again;
my memory of you outlasts my fate.

The Bottle

Some very strong perfumes can last for years;
some seem able to penetrate thick glass,
and so, opening a cask from the East
and the lock snags, then opens with a creak,

or in an empty house – the cupboard full
of time's smell, otherwise dusty and dull;
it's there you'll find an old bottle –
and from out of it springs a living soul.

Like chrysalids, a thousand sleeping thoughts,
trembling and fragile, dazzled by the light,
open their wings, stretch, then launch into
the air, all glazed with pink and gold and blue.

Memory whirls and spins through troubled air;
eyes close as vertigo grabs hold of a
poor soul in both hands and pushes it down
a stinking pit of human corruption.

On a bank by the side of this hell hole,
Lazarus tears his shroud; the stink is foul.
His actions cause another corpse to move;
he's woken up one of my ancient loves.

And in this way, I'll be forgotten soon,
left to rot in whatever drawer I'm thrown,

an decrepit old bottle, unwanted,
dusty, dirty, abused, cracked and haunted.

Now I'll be your coffin, you pestilence,
proof of your force and virulence,
you poison, made by angels, drop by drop,
so powerful, you forced my heart to stop!

Poison

Wine makes the most disgusting of hovels
                look rich with luxuries,
and causes magical porticoes to rise
                in mists of red and gold,
like the sunset in evening's misty skies.

Opium expands the boundless frontiers,
                lengthens the unmeasured;
slows time and provides many dark pleasures,
                negates all childish fears
and fills the soul with nebulous treasures.

All this – nothing to the poison that flows
                out of your green eyes – cursed
waters where my soul sees itself reversed...
                and my dreams always go
to those bitter waters to quench their thirst.

All this – nothing to your envenomed breath;
                your mouth's acidity,
that drowns and burns and eats away at me,
                and then, smiling like death,
drives me to nothingness, remorselessly.

Troubled Sky

Once more your eyes are troubled – a mist veils
their colour and your mood – their cruel grey,
the green that lights them up when you are shy,
the dreamy blue's reflection of the sky.

When I think of those faded, hazy days,
my heart relaxes, pain dissolves away,
and foreboding that remains undefined
jangles my nerves and unsettles my mind.

Sometimes you look just like the horizon
illuminated by an autumn sun;
a soaked countryside, glistening for my eyes,
glowing with diffused rays from troubled skies.

Dangerous and stormy woman, you know
how much I adore your frost and your snow;
can I now take from your cold winter's vice,
pleasures much sharper than iron or ice?

The Cat

1

A cat is strolling through my thoughts
and seems to think she is at home;
she's beautiful and likes to roam
around the place, her mewing soft.

Her voice is tender and discrete;
no matter whether quiet or loud,
it's always rich, always profound.
This is her charm and her secret.

She has a purr that makes its way
down into my heart – it's sublime,
thrilling me like a measured line
of verse; a drug that slows the day,

or numbs the cruellest agonies.
She never uses any words,
but every phrase of hers is heard;
each one contains pure ecstasy.

But no violin note could cut
my heart the way her perfect voice
does – she's a Stradivarius;
a tuned musical instrument.

And she sings with a royal voice,
one in which every angel-like
quality is strange, seraphic,
so subtle, and harmonious.

2

One evening I stroked her brown fur
gently with my careful fingers,
and I found her perfume lingered
long after I'd stopped stroking her.

Familiar spirit of the house;
she judges, presides, she inspires
and carefully rules her empire;
perhaps a god or something else?

When my bewitched eyes turn to see
this beloved cat, as though drawn
by a magnet, her eyes return
a reflected image of me.

I'm constantly amazed to see
the fire burning in her green eyes;
those living opals, those shining lights
that stare at me so steadily.

The Beautiful Ship

Soft enchantress, I want to tell the truth
of the pleasures that created your youth;
to tell of your beauty's
child-like charm and adult maturity.

Your skirt brushes the air in pleated whirls;
you're a beautiful ship sailing the world,
led by an offshore breeze,
following the soft, slow rhythms of the seas.

Fine shoulders, firm neckline, a regal face,

your perfect head held high – your inner grace;
and yet, triumphantly,
majestic child, you still go your own way.

Soft enchantress, I want to tell the truth
of the pleasures that created your youth;
to tell of your beauty's
child-like charm and adult maturity.

Pushing at your silk top, your thrusting breasts,
now transformed into a perfect sea chest,
those swelling panels that
curve delicately and reflect the light.

Enticing shields, armed with twin tips of rose!
stores of sweet secrets, too many to choose;
of perfumes, liqueurs, wines,
enough to distract the strongest of minds.

Your skirt brushes the air in pleated whirls;
you're a beautiful ship sailing the world;
led by the offshore breeze,
following the soft, slow rhythms of the seas.

Beneath your skirt, your legs move perfectly,
firing my desire and arousing me;
you're a witch who stirs up
aphrodisiacs in her magic cup.

Your strong arms could strangle young Hercules,
and teach the boa constrictor how to squeeze;
you hold your lovers tight
enough to imprint them upon you heart.

Fine shoulders, firm neckline, a regal face,
your perfect head held high – your inner grace;
and yet, triumphantly,
majestic child, you still go your own way.

Invitation to a Voyage

My child, my sister,
let us be together,
on a perfect island across the sea.
At leisure, you and I,
to live and love and die,
in lands that look like you, when loved by me.

The sun shining up high
in heat-hazed tropic sky
has an insistent, strong hold over me;
it has the mysteries
of your mischievous eyes,
that pour out their crystal tears so freely.

where everything is beauty, love and right,
luxury, calm and sensual delight.

Carved wooden furniture,
polished by passing years,
fills up our rooms. Among the ornaments,
the rarest plants and flowers
mingle their fragrances
with a faint and alluring amber scent.

The rich embossed ceilings;
the mirrors, revealing
the natural treasures of the Orient,
and if they could, they would
speak to our secret souls
in a language of native innocence,

where everything is beauty, love and right,
luxury, calm and sensual delight.

In harbours and canals,
ships and boats rest their sails,
their gypsy spirits stilled, their pennants furled,
and it is to fulfil
your needs, desires – your will,
that they've come from the far ends of the world.

Each day the setting sun
bathes fields, house and inns;
the streets of the entire city in gold
and hyacinth and rose.
The city's in repose
in a warm light that cherishes and holds,

where everything is beauty, love and right,
luxury, calm and sensual delight.

The Irreparable

1

How can we smother this old worm Remorse,
that lives and moves and writhes,
and feeds on us though we are a corpse;
a grub on new oak leaves?
How can we smother this old worm remorse?

What wine, cocktail, chemical, opiate,
to drown this false one in,
this greedy and destructive prostitute,
who's patiently waiting,
with wine, cocktail, chemical, opiate?

So tell me lovely witch, what I must do
to ease this pain? I feel
like a dying man crushed by the wounded,
disembowelled by steel wheels,
so tell me lovely witch, what I must do?

A wolf can always smell a dying man;
it's meat the crows will have;
once a praying soldier, now forgotten,
without a cross or grave,
and wolves can always smell a dying man.

Whatever power can light a darkened sky –
one that's blacker than tar?
No morning or evening; everyone blind
to winter lights and stars;
no power left to light a darkened sky.

At the inn, all our hopes were snuffed right out;
       all killed outright. Dead.
Out on the road there's no pale moon to light
       the way to a safe bed.
At the inn, all our hopes were snuffed right out.

So, sweet sorceress, do you love the damned,
       and do you know Remorse?
It has a bow and arrow and it's aimed
       at every man who's cursed.
So, sweet sorceress, do you love the damned?

Immortal souls are chewed by the cursed jaws
       of the Irreparable.
It attacks them from beneath, destroying floors
       and walls – it's terrible.
Immortal souls are chewed by the cursed jaws.

2

– I've seen all of this falsity before.
       It's just illusion.
Someone magical always ends a war;
       a miraculous dawn.
– I've seen all of this falsity before.

A being made of light and gold and gauze
       has Satan overthrown…
I wait for such an ending, but the pause
       is longer than I've known…
A being made of light and gold and gauze?

Conversation

You are a beautiful pink autumn sky,
but sorrow in me rises like the tide,
and when it flows away, eventually,
the memory's of stinging salt, now dried.

– It's no use stroking my chest with warm hands;
my heart was pulled out by a woman's teeth
and claws, some years ago, you understand?
She fed it to her favourite wild beasts.

My heart's a palace ransacked by the crowd,
who brawl and drink and kill and shout too loud...
– A perfume swims around your naked breasts!...

Beauty, you scourge of souls, it's your desire
to use your eyes to light festival fires,
so burn these scraps not wanted by the beasts!

Autumn Song

1

Soon I will be in cold darkness again
for that brief, lovely summer's quickly gone;
it's with a shock I hear the resounding
thuds of chopped logs echo on cobblestones.

My mood is wintry – I know so well
this sadness, anger, hatred, horror, shock,
and, like the sun trapped in a frozen hell,
my heart is no more than a red iced block.

I feel each cut log as it hits the ground;
each dying tree's scream cuts me to the core
my soul's a castle being attacked, and
the battering ram is smashing at the door.

I hear hurried hammer thuds nailing down
someone's coffin lid, but whose can it be?
Autumn's here for a while – summer has drowned;
those bright, hot days are now a memory.

2

Although I love your green eyes' lovely light,
today tastes quite bitter, my sweet beauty,
and nothing – not love or bedroom delights,
mean as much as the sun's rays on the sea.

But please love me tenderly; a mother
will always love a most ungrateful son,
a sister loves her prodigal brother;
sweet autumn is fed by the setting sun.

Make haste! The eager grave is waiting yet!
and let me rest my face between your knees,
tasting those torrid summers of regret;
the golden sweetness of the season's lees!

For A Madonna

Ex-voto in the Spanish style

I'll build for you, Madonna and mistress,
an altar in the depths of my distress.
Deep down in the hollow of my sad heart,
far from desire and every mocking glance,
I'll make a niche, enamelled gold and blue,
in which I'll stand a stone statue of you.
And with entwined polished poetic lines
inlaid with care inside my crystal rhymes,
I'll fashion for your head a giant crown.
And as I'm jealous, with my jealous frowns
I'll make a gown for you that you will find
barbaric, stiff, heavy, suspicion-lined,
to cover up those charms I hold so dear,
then I'll embroider your gown with my tears!
With my desire, I'll make for you a dress,
To fit tight to, and kiss the nakedness
of your contours – there's harmony, repose
and joy in your naked whiteness, your rose.
Respectfully, I'll make you satin shoes
and then humbly slip them over your toes,
and for that moment, while I'm feeling bold,
I'll trap your feet within my gentle hold.
I'll also try, for you deserve the best,
to let you use the moon as a footrest,
and if I fail, I'll find instead the snake
that eats my innards – you could always break
its spine under your feet. You can redeem
my soul by neutralising it's venom.
My thoughts, like tall church candles, can be seen

lit on the alter of my Virgin Queen
starring the blue ceiling with reflections,
while my awed eyes gaze at your perfection.
As I cherish you, worship and admire,
everything turns to incense and to myrrh
that rises to your white, snowy summit;
a mist that contains my stormy spirit.

Finally, to fulfil your role of Mary
and to mingle love with barbarity,
from the seven deadly sins, I have made,
like a mad killer, seven deadly blades
so razor-sharp they catch the flickering light;
and now you're stripped and tied, your bindings tight,
I'll throw at the target these seven darts
and they'll enter your red and streaming heart.

Afternoon Song

All of those mysterious looks
on your face made me think that you
were an angel, but now I know
that you're a witch with spells and hooks.

And I adore you, perfect one,
with a terrifying passion,
and with the same deep devotion
that a priest has for an icon.

Your lovely mane of gypsy hair
is scented with desert and woods;
your head's full of the attitudes
and enigmas you hold in there.

A rich scent comes from your body
as though from a censer; your charms
are those of a evening nymph, warm
and somehow subtly shadowy.

Nothing's as strong as your sex games,
not any drug cocktail or drink;

your soft touch has me on the brink…
You'd bring the dead to life again!

Your back, your hips, your waist, your breasts
and their pink roses, your smooth thighs;
your poses and the way you lie
excite cushions you rest against.

To appease your strange appetites,
when your moods make you laugh and cry,
you start to kiss me solemnly,
then change them to erotic bites.

Sometimes you heal me, then you hurt;
you laugh a scornful laugh that mocks,
and then you give a loving look –
one gentler than autumn moonlight.

And now beneath your perfect feet,
beneath your softest satin shoes,
I place with care – I offer you
my genius, my destiny.

You're a soul of colour and light
and with your heat I would be cured,
so please explode volcanic fire
in my deep Siberian night!

Sisina

Here's Diana, coursing through the forests,
disturbing brush, wearing her hunting gear,
dizzy from running, windswept hair, bare breasts,
more determined than her trained cavaliers.

Here's Théroigne, the lover of carnage,
inciting the barefoot mob to resist,
eyes bright, playing at war as though on stage,
climbing the royal stairs, sword in her fist.

Here's Sisina, she's such a gentle knight;
she can love and kill. Military drum
beats give her strength; battle sounds cause delight.

By all good soldiers, she can be disarmed,
but in her heart, withered by battle flame,
she keeps a lake of tears for the unharmed.

Praises for my Francisca

I need new strings to praise
you, graceful one, who plays
in my lonely heart's maze.

Laurels interwoven,
around you, sweet woman,
absolve you of all sin.

Your kiss rejuvenates
and burns me with its heat;
like the Lethe, it's sweet.

When I indulge in vice
and end up on thin ice,
you appear, sweet goddess.

You're brighter than the stars
and every waking hour,
I'm subject to your power.

You sweet pool full of virtue;
fount of eternal youth,
you've put love in my voice.

You've burned away the wrong,
you've helped the odd belong
and made the weak ones strong.

In hunger you're my bread,
in mazes you're my thread;
you're always my sweet guide.

Revive my sexual power,
bathe me a scented showers,
lay me in perfumed bowers.

Come, guard my loins from harm,
dress me in magic charms,
have angels stand by, armed.

Rock to precious sapphires,
bread to ambrosia,
fine wine, my Fransisca.

For A Creole Lady

In perfumed lands with warm and sunny skies,
I've known, beneath deep purple canopies
of palms that shaded brightness from my eyes,
a Creole lady's depths and mysteries.

Her skin was light and warm, an enchantress
with gentle ways that were almost royal;
tall and svelte, she walked like a lithe huntress,
with an assured gaze and a tranquil smile.

Lady, if you ever visit this land,
to walk by the Seine or the green Loire,
all will see your beauty and understand,

for in peaceful gardens, you have inspired
a thousand sonnets praising your glory,
by poets enslaved by your eyes' bright fire.

Sorrowful and Wandering

Tell me, does your heart sometimes fly away,
far from the black of the squalid city
towards a sea of exploded splendour,
blue, bright, profound, deep as virginity?
Tell me, does your heart sometimes fly away?

The sea, the vast sea, consoles our labours.
Whatever made the singing sea's voice hoarse,
accompanied by immense groaning winds,
with the sublime function of cradling us?
The sea, the vast sea, consoles our labours.

Transport me, wagon! carry me, frigate.
Far! far! for here mud is made of our tears!
– Is it true sometimes your sorrowful heart
says: Far from remorse, crimes, sufferings, fears,
transport me, wagon, carry me, frigate?

How distant you are, perfumed paradise,
where love and joy grow under azure light,
where all of those worthy of love are loved,
where pure hearts drown in sensual delight?
how distant you are, perfumed paradise?

But that green paradise of childish loves;
its rides, its songs, its kisses, its bouquets,
the violins vibrant amongst the hills,
with the jugs of wine, at evening, in the glades,
– yes, that green paradise of childish loves.

Innocent place, full of furtive pleasures,
how far beyond India and China?
Can we recall it with our plaintive cries,
bring it to life with a voice of silver,
that innocent place of furtive pleasures?

The Ghost

Like an Angel with eyes that burn,
it's to your bedroom I return
and float towards you as silent
as the dark shadows of the night.

I offer you, my dusky one,
my kisses colder than the moon
and the caresses of a snake,
coiling slowly around a grave.

When morning lifts its livid head,
you'll find me absent from your bed,
my place cold until night draws near.

Let others reign by tenderness,
over your life, your youthfulness;
myself, I want to rule by fear.

Autumn Sonnet

Your eyes speak to me, sparkling like crystal:
"My strange lover, what attracts you to me?"
– Be sweet and still! Everything annoys me,
except the candour of all animals.

My heart can't show secrets, and it will keep
the blackened legend written in its fire.
To you who gently soothes me into sleep,
I hate passion and never feel desire!

let's love gently – love's hiding somewhere near,
in ambush, waiting, taking careful aim
with all its weapons – the knives, guns and spears

of crime, horror, madness, fear and deceit.
I hope you are, like me, an autumn sun,
my icy, remote, cold, white Marguerite?

Sorrows of the Moon

Tonight, the moon is languidly dreaming;
a beautiful woman stretches on deep
cushions, and with a distracted light hand
caresses her own breasts before she sleeps,

Spread out upon that satin avalanche,
as though in a deep faint, she's mesmerised
by all the light, white visions that she sees
rising like flowers into the deep night skies.

70

And when, by chance onto the earth, there falls
a pure and rare and secret opal tear,
a watchful man catches that rainbow gem

in the warm hollow of his hand, and then
carefully hides that fading tear away
in his heart, far from the eyes of the sun.

Cats

Austere scholars and ardent lovers too,
equally love, in their maturity,
powerful and soft cats, pride of the house,
who like a warm fire and serenity.

They love the body's joys, they love the mind,
they seek the silent horror of the dark;
the devil wants them as funeral clerks,
but too proud for slavery, they decline.

In their dreams they have the same attitude
as the great sphinx stretched out in solitude,
seeming to sleep inside an endless dream;

their loins are full of sparks, all magical,
and flakes of gold, like finest sand are seen,
within those eyes that see the mystical.

The Owls

Under black yew trees, in the shade,
the owls have ranged themselves apart,
and in the manner of strange gods,
dart their red eyes. They meditate.

And there they stay without movement
up to the melancholy hour
when, blotting out the oblique sun,
darkness establishes its power.

The sage learns from their attitude;
in this strange world he'll need to shun
the violence and the multitude;

the man who enjoys the shadows
will always suffer punishment
no matter where on earth he goes.

The Pipe

I am the pipe of an author;
you can see, looking at my face,
dark as some Abyssinian race,
my master is a great smoker.

When he is overworked and tired,
I'm a kitchen chimney, smoking
with food that's cooked for the return
of the labourer from the field.

I enlace and embrace his soul
in the delicate net of blue
that rises from my mouth of coal.

I'm a powerful remedy
for the hurt in his heart, a charm
for his anguish and his worry.

Music

When music affects me like a great sea,
   I sail away
through mist towards the faintest star I see –
   without delay.

With clean, salt-filled sea air I fill my lungs
   and feel free;
over the backs of waves I ride and plunge –
   they carry me.
Within me are the suffering passions

of straining ships;
the winds, the storms, the swells, the convulsions

of immense deeps
rock me, or it's the mirror of my own
desolation.

Burial

If on some heavy-shadowed night
a charitable Christian soul,
behind piles of old debris, might
drop your body down some rat hole,

and at the hour when the stars, chaste,
close their eyes tight against the dawn,
the spider weaves her web in haste,
and the viper births her spawn;

you will listen to all the years
hanging over your condemned head;
to lamentable howls of wolves

and of the scrawny sorcerers,
the frolics of lecherous old men
and the plots of black marketeers.

A Fantastic Engraving

This spirit has nothing at all to wear,
except a crown won at some frightful fair,
grotesquely perched atop his skeleton.
without spurs or whip, he drives his phantom
horse fast – a beast apocalyptic,
panting and snorting like an epileptic.
They both traverse the depths of endless space,
trampling infinity with a reckless pace.
This soldier, brandishing a flaming sword,
goads his fierce mount to crush the nameless horde,
and like a prince inspecting his domain,

a cold cemetery, a horizonless plain,
where lie, with a lifeless sun overhead,
from ancient and modern history – the dead.

A Joyful Death

In rich, fertile earth full of snails, I come
to dig myself a very spacious grave,
where I can leisurely spread my old bones
and sleep forgotten like a shark in waves.

I hate last testaments; I hate the grave;
I don't want any tears – I am owed none.
If still alive, I'd invite the raven
to peck my squalid corpse down to the bone.

Worms! Friends with no ears or eyes in your heads,
a free and joyful dead man comes to you;
philosophers of life, sons of decay,

pass through my rich ruins without delay,
and tell me if there is further torment
for this soulless corpse, dead among the dead!

The Cask of Hate

Hate is the cask of the pale Danaïdes;
angry revenge has arms both strong and red,
with which she throws into empty darkness,
great seas of blood and the tears of the dead.

This demon has made secret holes from which
will fly a thousand years of suffering;
when she decides to revive her victims,
she does so to squeeze the life out of them.

Hate is a drunk in a seedy taverna,
whose constant thirst is born in the bottle,
which multiplies like the Hydra of Lerna.
– But happy drinkers know their conqueror,

and Hate is dealt a most deserving fate:
to never sleep – to always stay up late.

The Cracked Bell

It's a bitter and sweet thing on winter nights,
sitting next to a fire that smokes and twists,
and memory slowly starts to rise up at
the voices of bells sounding in the mist.

Blessed is the bell with a vigorous throat
which, for its age, is still fit and alert,
faithfully pealing its religious chant;
an old soldier keeping watch in his tent!

Me, my soul's cracked, and in its apathy
it chants its chants and fills the night's cold air
with a weak, feeble voice that sounds to me

like the death-rattle of a wounded man,
bleeding beneath piled up bodies, who died,
unable to move, even though he tried.

Spleen (I)

Pluvius, rain god, cross with the city,
empties his urn in floods of cold and gloom
onto foggy streets; pours mortality
over the occupants of every tomb.

My cat, its litter lost, scratches the wall,
shakes its thin, mangy body without rest;
in the gutter, an old poet's soul calls
with the sad voice of a shivering ghost.

A great bell clangs, and a smoking log's whine
keeps falsetto time with a wheezing clock,
meanwhile, a foul-smelling card game goes on

(the legacy of an aged hydropic)

and the Knave of Hearts and the Queen of Spades
swap love stories – of loves now in the grave.

Spleen (II)

I've memories… I've lived a thousand years…

A huge chest of drawers stuffed with balance sheets,
with heavy locks of hair rolled in receipts,
with verses, love-letters, lawsuits, ballads,
holds fewer secrets than my sad mind holds.
It's an immense vault, a great pyramid,
that holds more dead than mass graves ever did.

– I'm a cemetery hated by the moon,
where my miseries, like the worms, commune
eagerly on the flesh of my dear dead;
a boudoir full of dead roses, all strewn
over the out-of-date clothing; a room
where fading pictures hang on fading walls
and faint scents linger in empty bottles.

Nothing now lasts like these long limping days,
when under the weight of the snow-bound years,
apathy becomes full-grown ennui
transformed, by time, to immortality.
– From now on, life, you're nothing more than stone,
shrouded by waves of fear, always alone…

A sphinx ignored by an ignorant world,
sunk at the bottom of Sahara sands
forgotten on the map. All you want is
to sing to the sun setting on the land.

Spleen (III)

I am like the king of a rainy land,
rich but impotent, young yet very old,
who, scorning the fawning of his teachers,
is bored with his dogs and other creatures.
Nothing cheers him, not game, not falconry,

not people dying by his balcony.
The grotesque ballads of his favoured clown
do not uncloud this sickly tyrant's brow;
his flower-draped bed transforms into a tomb,
and chambermaids, who find all kings handsome,
have no new revealing clothes to put on
to draw a smile from this young skeleton.
The jeweller who sculpts his gold never can
erase corrupt elements from this man,
and even baths of blood, Rome's heritage,
which the powerful recall in old age,
do not warm up this bloodless, numb body,
where flows the green water of the Lethe.

Spleen (IV)

Heavy, a lid, the low sky presses down
on the face of an agonised spirit,
holding at arm's length the horizon
and making sad days darker than the night.

The Earth is changed into a humid cell,
in which hope, like a frantic, captured bat
with timid wings, beats at the wet walls
and hits its head against the ceiling's rot;

The rain runs down the window, mimicking
a set of prison bars – and then it rains
hordes of deadly mental spiders that spin
their gossamer-thin webs deep in our brains.

And then the furious clashing of bells
resounds – a din that echoes off the sky,
scaring the spirits wandering the streets,
who wail and cry and tremble endlessly.

With no drum beat, proceeding silently,
a funeral procession of the dead
files its way slowly, mournfully through me,
then plants a black flag deep in my bowed head.

Obsession

The great woods frighten as cathedrals do,
they shriek their organ shrieks from their cursed hearts,
death-rattles sound in their grief chambers too –
an echo's *de profundis* counterpart.

The ocean's depths and waves and tides remind
me of the bitterness of victory
over all men; their humiliation
can be heard in the laughter of the sea.

I love the starless night – it pleases me;
no stars to speak the only language known
in a sky that is bare, dark and empty;

a black canvas on which are now painted
a thousand images straight from my mind;
all vanished ones, with looks I recognise.

The Taste for Nothingness

Poor soul, you once thought every fight was sweet,
when hope spurred you to everlasting fame –
but no longer, so rest now without shame,
old fighter, retirement is not defeat.

Rest for a while, my heart; sleep your brute sleep.

Defeated and weary, you're a pirate
for whom love and war do not mean a thing,
delightful music, soft voices that sing
will play no more, for they don't touch your heart.

For you, the spring has lost all of its scent.

Minute by minute, time takes all my time;
from these great heights I can see down below
a stiffening corpse, covered by constant snow –
no hut, no shelter, confused and snow-blind.

Please take me, avalanche, I hate this cold.

Alchemy of Suffering

One man lights nature up with his desire,
another fills creation with his grief;
while one wishes to live a life of fire,
the other wants to put an end to life.

You assist me, mysterious Hermes,
just as you also intimidate me –
thanks to you I'm King Midas in reverse,
a tragic alchemist, sad and lonely.

All I can do is change gold into lead,
and paradise into a living hell,
by making the clouds shroud the cherished dead.

It's there I find the body of the one
I once loved – and on this celestial
shore, I construct an elaborate tomb.

Sympathetic Horror

Tormented by your destiny,
what thoughts within your hollow soul
descend from a most livid sky,
to free you? Well, reply, you fool!

– I'm insatiable and avid
for the obscure and the unknown,
but I won't whimper like Ovid
when he was exiled out of Rome.

The skies are torn like the sea-shores,
the vast clouds are black with your grief –
they are the hearses of your dreams.

my pride is mirrored in your core
and your bright lights clearly reflect
a hell, to where my heart defects.

The Self-Punisher

for J.G.F.

Without hate or without anger,
just like a butcher I will strike,
as Moses struck the desert rock,
and in your eyes I'll see your tears.

The water of your suffering
will water my Sahara sands,
and far from hope and far from land,
in your sea of salt tears, I swim,

just like a ship taking to sea.
Just like a drum sounding a beat,
deep down inside my drunken heart
your sobs resound so beautifully.

But I am not the one wrong note
that's heard in a flawed symphony;
today, voracious irony
shakes me with a grip on my throat.

And in my blood there's black poison,
it's there in my harsh voice, growing;
I'm an evil mirror, showing
the harlot her own reflection.

I am the knife, I am the scar.
I am the blow, I am the cheek.
I am the limbs, I am the rack –
the victim and the torturer!

In my black heart I'm a vampire,
– outcast – one of the abandoned
who always laughs, but is condemned,
because he can't smile anymore.

The Irremediable

I

An Idea, a Form, a Being,
falls from the sky and is buried
in the muddy depths of the Styx,
far away from heaven's seeing;

a naïve Angel, travelling
is tempted by deformity,
then trapped in grim captivity;
a caught butterfly, struggling;

someone dragged down by a whirlpool
into the depths of sheer despair,
where rescue and pockets of air
whirl past, singing like crazy fools;

a bewitched man, who futilely
tries to avoid, then to escape
the place that's full of hungry snakes,
but who has no light and no key;

a descendant, who in despair
stands at the edge of a huge trench
and gags at the disgusting stench
that wafts up to his rail-less stair;

a place where monsters made of slime
stare at the cursed with night-black eyes,
a blackness filled with dread cries
of creatures that will eat your time;

a ship caught in the polar ice
as in a crystal trap,
looking for a way to go back,
but held there in a freezing vice.

– Simple emblems, perfect tableau
of fate – irremediable,
to show that the Devil does well
whatever he chooses to do.

2

Each heart becomes its own mirror,
when it sees the face of its youth,
a well of dark and lighted truth,
in which trembles a livid star,

a graceful torch of the devil,
an infernal beacon that shines
relief and glory on the mind
– the conscience that's found in evil.

The Clock

Frightening, impassive, sinister – a clock,
whose threatening hands demand we: *"Remember!"*
Your heart's full of dread; fears without number
strike out and hurt with each resounding tick.

Pleasures vanish over the horizon,
like actors leaving the stage hurriedly;
each second eats another piece of joy
from man's allotted and earthly season.

Three thousand and six hundred times an hour,
Second whispers: *"Remember!"* – it's voice fast;
Now's insect voice says: *"I am in the past,
and through my foul siphon watch your life pour!"*

Remember! Souviens-toi! Esto memor!
(My metal throat speaks every known language.)
Don't waste a moment, mortal, learn to gauge
the richness of each time seam and its ore.

Remember that time is a skilled gambler
who always beats the wheel; he doesn't cheat.
The gulf is thirsty; sands of time run out;
the day winds down and night strikes; *remember!*

The hour will arrive when divine Fate,
when Virtue, once again your virgin bride,

when Repentance (the perfect place to hide),
will all say *"Die, old coward! It's too late!"*

PARISIAN SCENES

Landscape

So I can write my poetry, my verse,
I need to be high up, among the stars,
my chin in my hands, here in my attic
looking down on Paris, its streets and talk;
to hear the bells chime on the hour for me
and look at out the landscape when I please,
see drainpipes, towers, aerials, spires and beams
touching the skies over this city's dreams.

Through the mist the first star begins to glow
high in the sky, a lamp in my window;
columns of smoke rise up in feathered plumes,
the city's bathed in pale light from the moon.
Spring and summer and autumn come and go;
when winter brings the harsh and driving snow,
I'll shut the blind and draw the curtains tight
and build fantastic castles in the night.

I'll dream of perfect sapphire horizons;
of fountains weeping blue tears; of gardens
where lovers kiss and birds sing constantly –
an idyll created most lovingly.
If, outside my window, riots ensue,
I won't break off from what I have to do,
for I am deep in sensual delight
of evoking the Spring with all my might;
I'll gently pull a sun out of my heart,
and make the blue sky burn gold with my art.

The Sun

In this suburb, shutters are hung on shacks,
concealing multitudes of furtive acts.
and the sun with a cruel, redoubled heat
sears the city and fields, the roofs and wheat,
and I practise my swordsmanship alone,
finding in everything the chance of rhyme,
stumbling on words like jutting paving stones
and finding lines I've dreamt of many times.

Anaemia's enemy, the sun's gold yield
wakes up the worms and roses in the fields;
vaporises our fears, lightens the sky,
and fills our minds, like hives, with rich honey.
He rejuvenates the lives of cripples,
making them as supple as teenage girls;
makes harvests fertile, feeding everything,
so every heart can beat strongly and sing.

And when, like poets, he visits cities,
he gives a beauty to the vilest things;
an unannounced king without bodyguards,
he'll visit hospitals and old back yards.

To a Red-Haired Beggar-Girl

Pale girl with russet hair,
with holes in what you wear,
showing your poverty
      and your beauty.

For me, poet of shame,
your young and sickly frame
is brushed with light freckles
      and tenderness.

You move more gracefully
than any Roman Queen
in your velvet costume
      and heavy shoes.

In place of rags too short,
let a fine cloak from court
trail with loud and long pleats
      over your feet;

holed stockings show your thighs
to every lecher's eyes;
the gleam of a gold knife
      catches the light.

Let loose your ragged frills
and to our gaze reveal

your breasts, whose splendour tries
        to match your eyes.

As for your other charms,
you'll need to use your arms
to bestow heavy blows
        on groping rogues.

Despite huge pearls that glow;
sonnets by young fellows,
new suitors every day
        are sent away.

Mediocre rhymers too
dedicate works to you,
as other men unseen
        make you their Queen.

Young pages, struck by chance,
and lords, too old to dance,
look long to recompense
        some small expense!

You've counted in your bower
far more kisses than flowers,
and due to all your rules,
        you enslave fools!

– But still you scrounge and beg
for any scraps or dregs,
and outside kitchen doors,
        take less for more.

You glance surreptitiously
at the cheapest jewellery,
which I can't, to be fair,
        now let you wear.

No ornament at all,
no perfume, diamonds, pearls,
for your thin nudity,
        o my beauty!

The Swan

for Victor Hugo

1

Andromache, I think of you. This small stream
is a sad mirror, in which there appears
the majesty of your proud widowed pain;
it's a false Seine filled with your bitter tears,

and it inspires my fertile memory
as I walk through new-built sections of town.
Old Paris is no more – all city's change
faster than any mood-swings I have known.

And now the place is full of workmen's shacks,
of heaps of columns and grey concrete blocks,
and weeds, and stoneworks made green by puddles,
and, reflected in glass panes, strewn bric-a-brac.

Long gone now, there was a menagerie,
not far from which I saw, at that bright hour
that most work begins and all the busy
street dustcarts swirl their dust into the air,

a swan that had escaped from its small cage.
On the dry pavement, it rubbed its webbed feet,
trailing its white plumage over rough ground,
looking for dried-up streams, opening its beak

and nervously beating wings in the dust,
its heart still full of its blue natal pool,
thirsting for water, hoping for a storm –
I can still see this strange, mythical fool,

beneath the sky, like one of Ovid's myths,
stretching its trembling neck and eager head
towards an ironic, cruel blue heaven,
as if directing a reproach at God!

2

Paris changes, but my dark mood remains.
New buildings, scaffolding, flats, parking zones,
old suburbs redesigned – everything changed.
My memories are heavier than stone.

And by the Louvre, an image saddens me:
I think of the swan; its ridiculous,
sublime movements and strange gestures – exiled
in a dead city – then I think of you,

poor Andromache, torn from your lover's arms,
cruelly enslaved by arrogant Pyrrhus,
you crouch, head bowed, next to an empty tomb,
widow of Hector, grieving for your loss.

I think of a negress, consumptive, thin,
tramping through mud, and looking with tired eyes
for absent Africa's coconut trees,
through a vast mist that blocks out all the sky.

I think of those who've lost what can't be found,
ever; of those who drink their own hot tears
and feed the hungry wolf of suffering;
of orphans dying like beheaded flowers.

Deep in the woods where my soul wanders, lost,
a memory sounds like a hunting horn.
I think of voyagers left on an isle,
captive, defeated, broken... or much more.

The Seven Old Men

for Victor Hugo

Great swarming city, city full of dreams,
where stroller's sleeves are tugged by daylight ghosts,
and where each new mystery flows into
the many veins of this colossal host.

Early in the morning – I was alone
out on an empty, dingy, silent street,
the houses were wrapped in distorting mist –
just like a gothic film studio set;

a dirty yellow mist flooded the place.
I made my way, each noise jarring my nerves
as I passed through suburbs I did not know,
the streets were shaken by heavy vehicles.

Then an old man in scruffy yellow rags
the same colour as the mist and the sky
– who looked as though he deserved charity,
except for the nasty glint in his eyes –

appeared quite suddenly in front of me.
He stared at me without a single word,
his pupils looked like they'd been soaked in bile,
his Judas beard stuck out like a sharp sword.

He wasn't just bent, but broken, his spine
and legs forming a perfect right-angle,
and with his heavy stick, he had the look
and clumsy manner, awkward and tangled

of a sick creature left in a closed zoo.
But on he came, in snow and mud and strife,
as if he crushed the dead under worn shoes,
hating, but not indifferent to, life.

His double followed: rags, beard, back, stick, eye,
from the same mould; no differences were shown;
a pair of baroque ghosts, or ancient twins,
walking together towards the unknown.

What conspiracy had I discovered?
What tricks of fate were these? What cloning crimes?
As seconds passed, that sinister old man
multiplied his vile old self seven times!

To those who'd laugh at my horror and fear;
the fearless, the stupid, the sceptical,
know this: those seven ancient monsters were
creatures from the depths of the eternal.

Frightened, sweating, I knew I couldn't stay
to see another of those fatal twins
appear – and survive. My nerves torn away,
I turned my back on all of them and ran.

Bewildered, like a drunk who sees double,
I dashed home, shut my door, my sanity
completely in doubt, my senses troubled
by what I'd seen and its absurdity.

Vainly, my reason tried to find a hold
on nothingness – a tempest stormed my mind;
my thoughts were spun fast, like a crewless ship
on a sea lashed by storms that never end.

The Little Old Women

for Victor Hugo

1

In the oldest of the city's maze-like streets,
where everything's enchanting, even crime,
obeying my mood, I pause to observe
decrepit creatures, possessed of a strange charm.

Misshapen monsters that were once women,
now dressed in drab rags, in cold cloth tatters,
deserving of love, these poor, old lost souls,
broken, crippled, hunched, crooked and battered.

Lashed by a harsh North wind, they creep along
and tremble at each passing lorry's roar,
each with a small bag held tight to their sides
and embroidered with strange symbols and flowers.

They trot along the streets, broken puppets,
or drag themselves, like wounded animals;
it's as though they're dancing against their will;
as if some demon's ringing broken bells.

They've piercing eyes that drill straight through the skull,
gleaming brightly like deep holes in the night;

sparkling eyes, like those of a little girl
who laughs at things that give her most delight.

It can be seen that coffins of the old
and of children are often the same size.
This is the equality in death we've
heard of so often – the eternal prize.

Sometime I think about geometry
and the contorted limbs of these beings,
and how often workmen would need to change
each coffin's shape to put their bodies in.

So when I see one of these frail ghosts
make her way through Paris's swarming hordes,
I always think of her as looking for
a box, in which she can rest from the world.

Those eyes are wells full of a millions tears,
they're crucibles in which cold metal shines,
they're eyes of mystery; eyes of strange charm
for anyone in love with misfortune.

2

Vestal virgins guarding houses of vice;
former priestesses of temples, now free
of your forgotten names; each of you lost
women, I give you brand new histories:

There's one made tough by working on the land,
and one, whose husband made her live in fear,
and one, with child, became a Madonna –
all of them made a river with their tears.

I love them all – even the ones who make
some sort of virtue out of suffering,
and ask that one day their devotion will
take them to heaven on huge rainbow wings.

3

Once or twice I've followed these old ladies,
particularly one, who, when the setting sun

made the sky red, as though soaked in new blood,
sat herself down on a park bench, alone,

to listen to a military band
playing its music in a lovely park,
to encourage men to join the forces,
as the burnished sunset evening grew dark.

This woman, upright, haughty and regal,
eagerly listened to the martial tune;
her eyes glittered like those of an eagle,
her head was bowed, as though she wore crown.

4

And so you make your way, without complaint,
through the city's chaos - you're quite at home,
former mothers, whores, saints, or whatever
you were, for your names are no longer known.

Once you had perfect grace, perfect glory;
now you're unknown. A drunk propositions
you as you hurry past; you're followed by
a grubby child who yells admonitions.

Shrivelled shadows, ashamed to exist, hunched,
afraid, pressed to the wall, you're destiny's
strange ones - ignored by almost everyone,
you are the debris of humanity.

From a distance, I watch you tenderly,
as you take steps on your uncertain feet;
I watch you as a father, and enjoy
your passions and your pleasures with delight.

I was there when you experienced first love,
I was there when you suffered empty days,
I enjoyed the vices you indulged in,
and enjoyed your virtues in the same way.

We're so alike, my ruined family.
Every evening, I say a sad goodbye
to you, thinking, by morning, you might be
in God's terrible claws, held steadily.

The Blind

It doesn't matter that they always stare;
they're shop dummies, strange and ridiculous,
frozen, terrible, like somnambulists,
darting their unlit orbs everywhere.

The divine spark has gone from their pale gaze.
They either stare at nothing or the sky,
as though the horizon's faded away,
or heads down, they avoid the street's heat haze.

As they cross an inner limitlessness
–a black relative of endless silence–
the city that surrounds them sings, plays, laughs.

As I drag myself on, more numb than they,
in love with pleasure and atrocity,
I ask: *What do they look for in the sky?*

To a Woman Passing By

Deafening, the street around me roared.
Tall, slim, in black, wearing a look of hurt,
a woman passed by, her delicate hand
carefully holding the hem of her skirt,

lithe, sinuous, a model's sculpted legs.
I stood, tense and witless, drinking my fill,
from eyes of pallid skies where storms begin,
of tenderness that snares, pleasure that kills.

A lightning flash... then night! – Fleeting beauty;
your briefest glance recharged the life in me –
now gone, you'll live on in my circuitry.

You're somewhere else! Perhaps not! I am! You,
unknowing of my life, and I of yours;
for an instant we joined – and we both knew.

95

The Skeleton Labourer

1

Buried below ground like mummies,
on dusty cellar shelves, are books
containing pictures that depict
in detail, strange anatomies.

Drawn by a skilled artist, their theme
is savage rawness turned into
exquisite beauty; they all show
a melding of content and form.

One of those pictures, still quite clear
shows gruesome horrors – skeletons
and gangs of men all flayed of skin,
digging away like labourers.

2

What strange harvest is it you farm,
you work-gang from the abattoir,
and by which farmer were you hired
to fill his waiting, empty barn?

I see the effort in your bones
and in your muscles, bare and stretched,
I see the land you excavate,
you weary, overworked, dead ones,

What this clear picture shows to us
is something that troubles us deep;
there might be no eternal sleep
in the grave, as has been promised,

and all things are false – even death,
and nothingness is nothing less
than a betrayal; loneliness
will keep us digging while we've breath.

We'll work to remove the earth's crust
with bare feet and a heavy spade,

that cuts us as we, unafraid,
drip blood on anonymous dust.

Evening Twilight

Friend of the criminal, evening arrives,
a loping wolf, the accomplice of thieves.
The sky shuts slowly, the lid of a chest
and restless men turn into savage beasts.

A pleasant evening ends a busy day;
the tired are pleased to put their work away,
calming agitation and soothing grief.
the gentle evening light provides new life
to students feeding facts into their heads,
and tired workman crawling into cold beds.

Meanwhile, old demons living in the air,
awake like businessmen, then start and stare
and in their hurried flight knock into doors.
Lit by lights that slowly flicker, the whores
parade themselves along the street,
an anthill opening many retreats;
abruptly stepping from unlit doorways,
like enemies attacking suddenly;
moving swiftly through this city of mud,
like worms feeding secretly on warm blood.

Here and there you hear the hiss of kitchen chores,
the theatre crowd's yells, the orchestra's snores;
inn tables, at which gambling's played all night,
are filling up with card sharps, cheats and tarts,
and thieves; the crafty, who never pause,
will soon begin their work, forcing the doors
and safes gently open, so they can pay
for girlfriend's treats; food for a few more days.

Take time, my soul, to reflect on this. Pause
and close your ears on all this raucous noise.
This is the hour that pain and hurt increase.
Evening twilight grips their throats; they finish

their lives and move towards a common grave;
hospitals are full of their cries. – Most have
no chance to return to their fragrant home
and an evening fireside, with a loved one.

Besides, most have not really known the joy
of home sweetness and have not lived fully!

The Game

In second-hand armchairs, the ancient whores
with too much make-up pose and leer and preen
eagerly, nodding their aged heads, making
their paste jewels catch the light, so they are seen.

Around the green baize tables are thin-lipped
faces, colourless lips and toothless mouths;
fingers cramping with arthritic seizures
search through a pocket or a sweat-stained blouse.

Beneath a filthy ceiling, rings of bulbs
in enormous chandeliers shine dim light
onto the sad faces of old poets
who've lost their spark and can no longer write.

And in my mind's eye I can see the shape
and details of a very recent dream:
I'm standing in a corner of this place,
cold, impotent, alone, wanting to scream,

and envying every other man's lust,
as they barter with old whores for a price
agreeable to both – one lusts for youth,
the other overlooks a life of vice.

I'm envious too, of the poor man who'll rush
into the void, find a false paradise
where blood is poisoned, preferring the risk
of pain to death and hell to nothingness!

Dance Macabre

for Ernest Christophe

Almost alive, proud of her model's shape,
her handkerchief, her gloves, her big bouquet,
her manner is offhand; the nonchalance
of an outrageous flirt with lavish ways.

No woman's waist has ever been so slim.
Her dress flows around her with regal power
and falls onto her feet, encased inside
her hand-made shoes, decorated with flowers.

And like a lust-filled stream rubs against rocks,
the frill that plays across her clavicles,
defends modesty from mass ridicule,
those charms her revealing clothes conceal.

Her deep eyes are empty, full of darkness,
and her skull, artistically arranged with pressed
flowers, nods gently on her fragile bones.
Her charm is nothingness, so strangely dressed.

Named as a caricature by a few
lovers of flesh, who do not comprehend
the unfleshed elegance of the human frame.
Your style is beauty, lovely skeleton.

When, troubling and powerful, you smile
at festivals of life, does some desire
inspire and invite your living carcass
to take part in a Sabbath of Pleasure?

Will songs, will violins, will candle flames
block out dream terrors mocking you at night,
or will you demand thousands of orgies
to cool the hell-made metal in your heart?

Primitive distillery of lasting pain.
Eternal well of folly and mistakes.
Along the curved trellis of your ribcage,
I see entwined an insatiable snake.

It's true, I fear your flirtatious nature;
it's strong and drives away all you would keep;
what mortal heart could ever stand your jokes?
The charms of horror are not for the weak.

The abyss of your eyes, full of grim thoughts,
exhales vertigo, and no skilled actor
could kiss you without feeling nausea
at the eternal smile of your locked jaw.

Yet, who's never embraced a skeleton,
or nourished themselves on things from the grave?
How important are clothes or perfume now?
How beautiful you make your grim display.

Noseless beauty, irresistible corpse,
those who cause you most offence, take to task:
"Proud darlings, despite make-up and perfumes,
You smell of Death, skeletons soaked in musk,

dandies with hairless faces, withered beaus,
fossilised Casanovas, made of bone,
the endless whirling of the dance macabre
hurls you into a place as yet unknown!

From Seine's cold quays to the Ganges' burnt sides,
this leaping, swooning mortal group don't see
an angel's trumpet in the sky, pointing
like a gun, aimed at them sinisterly.

In snow or sun, Death admires you
in your contortions, poor humanity
and often, like you, the perfume of myrrh,
blends your irony with your insanity!"

The Love of Illusion

You see me watch you dance nonchalantly,
as from the vibrant walls, soft music plays,
and slow your harmonious, alluring strut
and stare back with an apathetic gaze;

When I look at your delicate body,
your pallid charms enhanced by coloured lights,
it's as though evening's turned into new dawn
for your eyes become torches of delight.

I think: she's beautiful and innocent.
Her memories pile up like a tall tower
upon her head; her heart's bruised like a peach,
and is now ripe enough for a lover.

Are you an autumn fruit that tastes supreme?
Are you a funeral urn waiting for tears,
or perfume of distant oasis dreams,
a soft pillow, or a basket of flowers?

I know that there are some unhappy eyes,
that never hide precious secrets within;
caskets without jewels, jewels without stones,
as empty and as deep as a heaven.

But you look like an object of desire;
you're illusion, when most just want the true,
I don't care about your indifference,
I admire your mask's design and desire you.

'I have not forgotten...'

I have not forgotten our white house,
small and tranquil, but with the city close;
old statues of Pomona and Venus
hiding their nude limbs in a stunted copse.
The sun, in the evening, streaming warmly
upon the window, where it broke its rays,
seemed like a great eye in curious skies
watching us dine in delightful silence,
kindly spreading a candle glow on both
the thin curtain and frugal tablecloth.

'The kind servant, of whom...'

The kind servant, of whom you were jealous,
now sleeps beneath a humble patch of grass –
we really should have taken her some flowers.
The dead, the poor dead, have such great sorrows,
and when October, pruner of old trees,
blows sullen winds through marble cemeteries,
surely, they find the living such ingrates,
asleep, as they are, warmly in their sheets,
while, devoured by multitudes of blackest dreams,
with no bed-mates, with no good conversations,
old frozen skeletons riddled with worms,
can sense the winter snows as they disperse
and time passing; friends and family fail
to replace the scraps that hang on their rails.

If, one evening, when logs sizzle and sing,
I see her in the chair, calmly sitting;
if, on a cold, blue night of December,
I find her crouched in my chamber corner,
solemn, risen from eternity's truth,
to keep maternal eyes on this grown youth;
what should I say to this most pious soul,
as from its hollow eyes, many tears fall?

Mist and Rain

Dying autumn, dead winter, mud-drenched spring –
all hibernation seasons! Hear me sing
how they anaesthetise my heart and brain
in shrouds of vapours, tombs of mist and rain.

On this great plain, where mighty cold winds blow,
where through the long night all weather-cocks crow,
until the hour is reached for renewing,
and my soul opens wide its raven's wing.

Nothing is sweeter to the saddened heart
than being drowned deep in the frost and dark,
my queen of climates and seasons that fade.

The constant presence of your pallid shades,
will find, on moonless nights, both of us spread,
numbing our pain in our hazardous bed.

Parisian Dream

for Constantin Guys

1

There is a terrible landscape,
such as no one has ever seen;
again this morning, this image
overwhelmed me when it appeared.

Sleep is miraculous; in dreams
are methods most peculiar;
this fearful scene is now purged clean
of everything irregular.

A painter, proud of my talent,
I love my imagined picture,
a caught monotonous moment
of metal, marble and water.

A Babel of stairs and arcades,
a palace that is infinite,
full of blue pools with warm cascades
and burnished gold catching the light.

Where cataracts of waterfalls
make crystal curtains in the air
and hang suspended, as though walls
of pure metal are standing there.

No trees, but simple colonnades,
encircle lakes and flat stone shelves,
on which colossal naiades,
like mirrored girls, admire themselves.

Torrents of water pour forth, blue,
by quays of rose and emerald,

pushing a million ways on through
towards the edges of the world.

Magic waves and unheard of stones;
giant mirrors of perfection
hurt every eye by what is shown
in their surfaces reflection.

Insouciant and taciturn,
new Ganges' in the firmament,
pour out the treasure of their urns
into the gulfs of diamond.

Architect of my magic scenes,
I make it all with whim or will,
and through a jewelled tunnel, then
into an ocean it all spills.

And all, even the colour black,
seemed burnished, lit, or set to blaze;
liquid holding glory intact
within its myriad crystal rays.

There were no stars from anywhere,
no sign of the sun burning high
or low, with its intrinsic fire,
spinning in this amazing sky.

And over these moving wonders,
there's a terrible novelty
to be seen, but not to be heard –
the silence of eternity.

2

I woke up fast, my eyes burning
and viewed my drab room with horror.
I no longer felt the yearning
I'd felt – now there was just sorrow.

The clock struck noon with brutal chimes
and from the sky, darkness was hurled
down on me, who lived out my time
in a sorrowful and numb world.

Morning Light

Reveille sounds around the barracks square
and streetlamps flicker in the morning air.

It is the hour when dreams swarm free, wicked;
when adolescents stir in their warm beds;
when, like an eye that bleeds and throbs with pain,
the lamplight on the day makes a red stain;
when spirit, beneath its body's huge weight,
is like the light and dark locked in a fight;
when warm breezes blow every teardrop dry;
when air is full of trembling things that fly;
when man tires of writing, woman of love.

When from the chimneys smoke rises above;
when prostitutes, with dark shadowed eyelids,
mouths open, sleep a sleep heavy, stupid;
when freezing beggar-girls hug their thin forms
and blow on grubby fingers to keep warm.

It is the hour, among the cold and mean,
when women's labour pains become extreme;
when distant cockcrows rip mist's maidenhood,
like cries stopped by a throat of frothing blood;
when rough seas beat against the capital;
when dying men laying in hospital
utter their death rattles in ragged gasps;
when party-goers, tired, return at last.

Dawn shivers in a dress of rose and green,
advancing slowly on the empty Seine,
and sombre Paris, rubbing sleep-filled eyes,
picks up tools, an old man, industrious.

WINE

The Soul of Wine

One evening, wine's soul sang in its bottles:
"Disinherited man, to you I send,
from my glass prison and vermilion seals,
a song full of light and fraternity.

I know how much you've worked the scorching hill;
what sorrow, sweat and burning sun you've found
to grow my life and offer me a soul,
and I am not ungrateful, nor unkind,

for I feel immense joy when I'm interred
in the throat of a man, worn by his work,
and his warm breast is a comforting bed,
where I prefer to be to my cold vault.

Do you hear them ringing out loud refrains
of hope that sing in my own trembling breast?
Elbows on the table and rolled up sleeves,
you glorify me and you will be blessed;

I'll light the eyes of your delighted wife;
to your son I'll give new force and colour,
and shall be, for this frail athlete of life,
the oil that strengthens the fighter's muscles.

In you, ambrosia is what I'll be,
precious grain of eternity's sower,
and from our love will grow new poetry,
thrusting to heaven like the rarest flower."

The Rag-Picker's Wine

During the red clarity of the night,
when winds rattle the rows of dead streetlights
and outcasts huddle in the cold doorways
of derelict buildings in a slum's maze,

a ragged man appears, shaking his head,
stumbling against the walls, like a poet,
and, uncaring of laughter, picks subjects
he loves to expound on – glorious projects.

He makes promises and dictates his rules,
relieves victims, terrorizes the cruel,
and underneath a sky of darkest blue,
grows drunk on the strength of his own virtue.

Harassed by domestic concerns, this man,
ground down by age and work, still somehow stands
exhausted, bent by the ragged debris
and rubbish spewed by enormous Paris.

He finds a home, perfumed with alcohol,
followed by friends, either white-haired or pale
grizzled and unshaven and battle-scarred.
Then suddenly, banners and flowers appear

right there, as though by some strong magic spell –
and at this deafening, dazzling festival
of bugles, cries, drums – of the sun above,
the happy people all get drunk on love!

This is the way with humanity, fickle,
as wine becomes a flowing gold trickle;
from a man's throat, of its exploits, it sings,
and reigns by the powers of the true kings.

To drown the anger and the insolence
of all the old ones, dying in silence,
God created sleep, touched by compassion;
Man added wine, sacred son of the sun!

The Murderer's Wine

My woman's dead, and I am free!
Now I can drink all that I want.

Once, I returned without a cent,
and her shrill cries tore right through me.

I am as happy as a king;
the air is pure, clear sky above...
That summer we first fell in love
was like this, I'm remembering!

In order to quench this raging
thirst that's tearing my throat, it would
take all the wine her tomb will hold;
and that's really saying something:

I found a drain and threw her in
and down onto her, I dropped all
of the stones from a nearby wall.
– I'm trying to forget her name.

In the name of all tender vows,
which nothing could ever untie,
I'd asked that we be reconciled,
just like our love's first time, somehow.

I implored her to meet with me
on a deserted road, one night.
She must have been quite mad, poor mite!
Well, we're all more or less crazy!

Although she looked a little strife-
worn, she was still pretty, and I –
I loved her too much, which is why
I ordered her: 'Out of this life!'

Nobody understands me. Did
one stupid drunkard ever dream,
during a night of morbid screams,
of making wine into a shroud?

This scum, this unfeeling machine
made of iron, emotions hindered,
never, in summer, nor winter,
has known a love that's genuine;

a love with deep, dark enchantments,
her infernal procession of fears,
her phials of poison, her hot tears,
her sounds of bones, her sounds of chains!

– As I'm now free and solitary!
Tonight I'll drink myself to death,
and sleep it off upon damp earth,
and without fear, without worry.

Like some old dog, I'll soundly sleep.
The vehicles, the big-wheeled trucks,
loaded with stones and sludge and muck,
the raging wagon may just keep

on crushing my culpable head,
or cutting my body in half;
I'll damn them all and loudly laugh
at devils, gods, at wine and bread.

The Solitary's Wine

An attractive woman's most candid gaze
as she glides by is like the pure white beam
of a pale moon cast on the rippling stream,
where, in her nonchalant beauty, she bathes;

the last bag of coins in the gambler's hands;
amorous kisses from some thin harlot;
music's enervating and tender notes,
as though humans uttered suffering sounds.

My dear bottle, none of these things are worth
the penetrating comforts you provide
for the humble poet's heart's raging thirst.

You're the treasure of the poor and the odd;
to them you pour out hope, youth, life, and pride,
and fill us with triumph – make us like gods.

The Lover's Wine

Today space is simply perfect.
Without spurs or bridle or bit,
let us gallop away on wine,
through skies enchanting and divine.

Like a pair of tortured Angels,
at the hands of callous strangers,
in morning's crystal blue distance,
we can pursue a lost mirage.

Gently balanced upon the wing
of an intelligent whirlwind,
in parallel delirium,

my lover, side by side we swim,
racing without rest or repose
towards our dream's own paradise.

FLOWERS OF EVIL

Destruction

A demon stirs constantly at my side;
sometimes he floats around me in the air
I swallow him and he sets me alight,
filling me with guilty, lasting desires.

And sometimes, knowing my great love of art,
he takes the form of women most seductive,
and, using the excuses of the false,
feeds me with drugs that are most destructive.

And from the sight of God, he pushes me,
gasping, broken and worn-out, to a land
of empty, wasted plains of apathy,

where he fills my eyes with great confusion;
of ragged clothing stained by open wounds;
the bleeding garments of the Destruction!

A Martyr

Drawing by an unknown Master

Surrounded by bottles and lamé swathes,
voluptuous furniture,
by perfumed robes with sumptuous pleats,
and oil paintings of nature,

in a tiny room, as in a greenhouse,
with air dangerously fatal,
from bouquets dying in their glass coffins,
as final breaths are exhaled,

a headless corpse floods out, in a stream,
onto the pillow, dark stains
of red, living blood, which the linen drinks
like a thirsty, sun-parched plain.

Like a pale vision born in the shadows,
that keeps the eyes enchained,

the head, with its piled dark mane of hair
and precious jewellery entwined,

rests on the nightstand, like a buttercup
in repose; empty of thoughts,
and from its rolled up eyes, a gaze escapes,
as vague and black as twilight.

On the bed, the nude body is spread out
in abandon and shameless,
showing its splendours; the fatal beauty
of its perfect naturalness.

On one leg is a gold-flecked pink stocking,
the garter, a souvenir,
looks with a diamond gaze through secret eyes
blazing with reflected fire.

This singular solitude, like a vast
portrait with enticing eyes
and a languorous pose, reveals a love
unspeakably based on lies.

Guilty joys and perverse entertainments,
hellish kisses of poison,
and through the tapestries there swarm
black angels all rejoicing;

and yet, one can see the elegant contours
of the shoulders lean and lithe;
sweetly rounded haunches, the playful pose,
like a snake prepared to strike.

She's still quite young! – Were her senses and soul,
chewed and eaten by ennui,
open to a baying pack of desires,
errant and lost and hungry?

Despite your love, that evil man you could
not, whilst living, satisfy,
did he, on your inert, compliant flesh,
his vast desires, gratify?

Answer! Did he grip your flowing tresses
in his feverish fist? Tell
me, gory head, did he, on your cold mouth,
place the ultimate farewell?

– Far from the impure crowd, the mocking world,
and curious magistrates,
strange creature, now sleep in peace, sleep in peace,
in your mysterious vault;

your bridegroom roams the world, and you stand guard
over him, watching his rest;
as much as you, no doubt, he is faithful
and constant even in Death.

Lesbos

Mother of Roman games and Greek delights,
Lesbos, where kisses, languorous, joyous,
decorate the days and the glorious nights,
warm as the sun and as fresh as new fruit,
mother of Roman games and Greek delights,

Lesbos, where kisses shower in cascades
violently down into the deep abyss,
the currents twisting, turning, unafraid,
swarming for an outlet, storm-lashed secrets,
Lesbos, where kisses shower in cascades.

Lesbos, where women seek other women out,
and to each sigh, another sigh responds,
it is a land of Paphos in the light,
where Venus and Sappho loosen their bonds,
Lesbos, where women seek other women out.

Lesbos, where nights are warm and languorous,
where girls with dark eyes gaze at their likeness
in mirrors, while their loving palms caress
and stroke their own sterile, yet longing thighs,
Lesbos, where nights are warm and languorous.

Philosophers cast disapproving eyes

on such delights – they're from excessive lust.
But you're queen of joys and appetites
that remain unknown, untasted by most;
philosophers cast disapproving eyes.

Your ambitions are martyred every day,
yet you're forgiven for your overreach;
your smile lights up a brand new morning sky,
that pinkly infuses the coral beach,
where your ambitions are martyred each day.

What god would judge you, or command you die,
or damn your pure brow with divine contempt?
Those golden scales have weighed the tears you cry,
and found you overcharged, without receipt.
What god would judge you, or command you die?

What is the point of laws of right or wrong?
Worshipped virgins, guardians of your isle,
you have your faith of love, the perfect songs
of your beliefs – no heaven or no hell;
what is the point of laws of right or wrong?

Lesbos chose me from everyone on Earth,
to sing the secret of her maiden flowers,
for as a child I shared the thrills, the birth
of happy laughter interspersed with tears.
Lesbos chose me from everyone on Earth.

I stand alone on the Leucate crags,
watching the sea with my vigilant gaze,
staring at every boat, knowing their flags
as they sail over calm blue, or through haze;
I stand alone on the Leucate crags.

To see if the sea's merciful and kind,
and if the rocks echo with living sobs,
now that Sappho's dead body is returned
to Lesbos, from the sea in which she drowned;
a sea that may prove merciful and kind.

Sappho, the poet and lover and man;
a woman with eyes flecked with black shadow,
more beautiful than Venus, sad and wan;

with eyes holding all that blue eyes don't know,
Sappho, the poet and lover and man.

More beautiful than Venus as she stands
naked, the world's admiring gaze on her.
The ocean's daughter, desired in all lands,
delightfully lit by the sun's gold fire,
more beautiful than Venus as she stands.

Sappho, who died on the day she blasphemed
against the cult's rites she had once bowed to,
her beautiful body was sacrificed
carefully, by some proud, arrogant brute;
Sappho, who died on the day she blasphemed.

Since then, Lesbos has cried a million tears,
while on that isle the world heaps with honours,
she spends each night tormented by the fears
that echo as cries on her barren shores;
since then, Lesbos has cried a million tears.

Condemned Women: Delphine and Hyppolyta

Lit palely by the lamps and languishing
on deep cushions imbued with incense,
Hyppolyta recalled the thrilling kiss
that stripped the veil of her young innocence.

She searched with eyes troubled by inner storms,
for the sky of her purity, long gone,
like a voyager who turns to look beyond
the morning's blue and distant horizon.

The lazy tears that dropped from her dazed eyes,
the voluptuousness, the look of stupor,
her conquered pose, arms lowered in defeat,
all served to emphasise her frail beauty.

Stretched at her feet, relaxed and full of joy,
Delphine observed her with her ardent eyes,
like a lioness devouring its prey
after its teeth have marked its fleshy prize.

Strong beauty kneeling before frail beauty,
superb, and breathing the voluptuous
wine of triumph, stretching towards her love,
as if to gather one more grateful kiss.

She gazed long into her pale victim's eyes,
hoping to find the songs of pure delight,
of gratitude for feeling the sublime,
beneath eyelids, half-closed in the dim light.

– "Hippolyta, my precious sweet one, now
you realise you've no need to perform
a sacrifice by offering your rose
to one who'd kill it with his violent storms.

My kisses are as gentle as mayflies,
caressing the lakes in the scented dusk,
but those of his are like deepest ruts,
gouged out by ploughs or steel wheels in the dust.

They'll drive over you, relentless, heavy,
without brakes, a merciless vehicle –
Hippolyta, look at me, please, my love,
my heart, my soul, my better me, my all,

and show me your eyes full of skies and stars,
for one divine look, one enchanting glance,
I'll lift the veil of unknown joys once more,
then let you sleep the sleep of the entranced."

But Hippolyta raised her troubled head
and said: "I'm not ashamed. I've no regrets,
Delphine, but I'm afraid, as though I've fed
on some strangely unique feast or banquet.

I feel a heavy dread fall over me,
as though I'm walking down a moving road
led by dark battalions of ghosts,
and shut in on each side by skies of blood.

Have we done something wrong or forbidden?
Why do I feel such terror and such fear?
For when you softly say "My love' to me,
my mouth moves slowly, wanting your lips near.

Please don't look at me like that, my delight,
my always lover, the sister I choose,
if you're the ambush that was set for me,
to love you is to win, to love you, lose."

At which tragic Delphine shook out her hair
and stood up, stamping her feet angrily.
"How dare you speak of losing when in love?
How dare you speak of loss when you have me?

I curse the dreaming man who caused this hurt;
the one whose vast and deep stupidity
has caused this puzzle to exist at all:
the one who mixed love with morality!

Any man who would join in harmony
those things not meant for joining – day and night,
summer and winter, hot and cold, will be
always useless – his body paralysed.

Go! Find a husband! Find some oafish man,
to give you love – let him greedily feast
upon you, doing everything he can;
you'll come back so I can bathe your scarred breasts.

Choose God or Mammon – you cannot serve both."
The grief-stricken girl, her mind torn between
her present and her future, cried aloud:
"The hugest void that I have ever seen

is opening in my soul. It is my heart,
burning like a volcano; a never-
satisfied monster, devouring my flesh;
a raging fury, burning forever.

Let these drawn curtains hide us from the world,
and let our tiredness bring us both some rest.
On your soft bosom, let me find peace, curled
up in the necropolis of your breasts."

Descend, you victims, pitifuls, descend
along the path of everlasting fire,
into the gulf of the most shameful crimes,
where all that's left are shadows of desire,

boiling to nothing, like a raging storm.
Whipped by a wind that never saw the sky,
your passions all remain unsatisfied,
and your past pleasures all wither and die.

No sunlight ever shone in this cavern,
although mists find ways through the rough stone walls,
and shed a sickly light – a lantern glow,
and poison your body with their rank smells.

The bitter taste of all your past delights
enflames your thirst and makes your parched skin sag,
the raging storm of your fierce appetites
blows against your frail flesh, like an old flag.

Far from the world, condemned and wandering,
across vast desert tracts, you run like wolves;
pursue your destiny, deranged spirits,
run from the infinite that's in yourselves.

Condemned Women

Like pensive cattle lying on the sand,
they turn their eyes towards the pale blue sea,
feet seeking feet, and their near-touching hands
are soft and languid, shaking bitterly.

Some, with hearts wrung by long private talks,
walk in the deep glades with the babbling streams,
and spell out their timorous girlish loves
by carving the wood of the young, green trees.

Others, like sisters, walk, so grave and slow,
among the rocks full of apparitions,
where Saint Anthony, rising slowly, saw
the naked, pale breasts of his temptations.

There are some, who, by lights of melting wax,
from the old pagan caves' hollow silence,
call out for help in their raging fevers,
"O Bacchus, duller of ancient remorse!"

And others, whose throats love the cutting blade,
conceal whips under their long robes, and then
in the wood's shadow of solitary night,
mingle pleasure's froth with tears of torment.

You virgins, demons, monsters, you martyrs,
spirits who hate the great reality,
seekers of the infinite, the satyrs
and saints, full of tears, full of agony,

you, who my soul has pursued to your hell,
poor sisters, I love you, but am pitiful
of your great suffering, your unquenched thirsts –
for your great hearts, the urns of love are full.

Two Good Sisters

Debauch and Death, both amiable girls,
lavish their intimacies upon me
while dressed in rags, and yet their virgin loins
remain barren throughout eternity.

The poet, enemy of families,
favoured in hell, a cheap-rate, rented whore,
has tombs and brothels show in tree-lined walks,
a bed that's unfrequented by remorse.

Coffin and bedroom, rich in blasphemy,
are offering, in turn, two good sisters,
terrible pleasures, hideous tenderness.

Debauch, when will your squalor bury me,
and you Death, when will you, rival mistress,
graft onto her myrtle your black cypress?

The Fountain of Blood

It seems, sometimes, my blood flows out in gobs,
the way a fountain spurts in rhythmic sobs.

I clearly hear its long murmuring sound,
but in vain I feel my body for a wound.

Through the city, it's a river enclosed,
that turns pavements to islands, as it flows,
quenching the thirst of every poor creature,
and staining everything the red of nature.

I've often demanded that the best wine
should numb each day this vast terror of mine;
with wine, the senses become newly-purged!

In deep, forgetful sleep for love I've searched;
but love is nothing but a bed of nails,
made to provide drink for the cruellest girls.

Allegory

This is a woman with a rich neck-line,
who lets her long hair fall into her wine.
No claws of love, no marks of vice and sin,
have marred the marble smoothness of her skin.
She laughs at death and mocks debauchery,
who scratch and pinch in their destructive play,
but whose talons never touch the majesty
of her lithe body, firm and straight and free.
She walks, a goddess, or a sultan's wife,
and feasts on pleasures from the tree of life;
her eyes impel the human race to rest
in her soft arms, upon her gentle breast.
She knows and feels, this wise, yet virgin girl,
the necessary workings of the world.
Her body's radiant beauty is sublime;
it pardons and forgives every crime.
She's never heard of hell or purgatory,
and when the darkness comes, she'll happily
look full into the pallid face of death,
without remorse or hate – an innocent.

My Beatrice

In a charred land, bereft of grass and trees,
as I moaned aloud at nature without cease,
wandering aimlessly, sharpening my thought's
blunt edge against the steel within my heart,
I saw a dark, storm-filled cloud, containing
a troupe of vicious demons, descending
towards my head. Like cruel and curious dwarfs,
they studied me coldly and then they laughed,
the way folk in the street laugh at those fools
who mutter, stumble, rant and rave and drool.
These beings nudged and winked and shook their heads
and whispered to each other, then they said:

– "Take your time looking at this caricature,
this false Hamlet, who mimics the posture,
the indecisive glance, the wind-swept hair.
It's such a shame this would-be millionaire,
this out-of-work actor, beggar and clown,
who once could play his roles with some renown,
should now try to impress, with long-dead powers,
the eagles and crickets, the stream and flowers,
and recite and bellow words not fit for swine,
at us, the authors of his ancient lines."

Right then (just as a matter of sheer pride),
I should have ignored what those demons cried;
I would have turned my back and walked away,
had I not seen among that crude display,
a crime that nearly cancelled out the sun!
My perfect queen, a beauty matched by none,
lifted her gaze and laughed at my distress,
then favoured each fiend with a soft caress.

The Metamorphosis of the Vampire

The woman, with her strawberry flavoured lips,
twisted and writhed her graceful, snake-like hips,
slipped off her silver top, thrust her breasts near,

124

and let her musk-soaked words flow in my ear:
"I have the warmest mouth, and know the skills
to make all men renege on their own wills.
I dry their tears on my triumphant breasts,
and help the old ones find their inner beast.
Naked, I am Salome without veils,
I am the moon, the sun, stars, comet's tails,
and am so learned in voluptuousness,
that when I entwine men between my thighs,
or else let them frenziedly bite my breasts,
the impotent, the virile, and the rest,
while in this bed, collapse contentedly,
for those poor angels give their best to me."

After she'd sucked the marrow out of me
and I had turned my body lazily,
to give her a long, probing and deep kiss,
a flask full of disease was suddenly
right there instead of her! I closed my eyes
and kept them shut until it grew quite light,
and then I looked, but she had gone for good;
no vampire lying next to me in bed,
instead, there were a skeleton's old bones,
that rattled like a metal weathervane,
or some old creaking sign, or sheets of tin,
throughout the day, blown roughly by the wind.

A Voyage to Cythera

My heart and a bird, joyously as one
circled above the rigging, free and high;
the ship rolled on under a cloudless sky,
an angel dazzled by a radiant sun.

What's that black island? – Cythera, they say,
sung of in songs and, according to lore,
the Eldorado of all bachelors –
a place that no sane man would want to stay.

– Isle of soft secrets and entertainments!
The primal shade of majestic Venus

drifted like perfume above azure seas
and filled the spirit with love's contentment.

The myrtle glades and flowers of the island
were praised by everyone from everywhere;
when adoring hearts sighed softly in the air,
it was like incense in a rose garden,

or the cooing of a dove during twilight!
– Now, Cythera is nothing but dead land,
where strange, sharp cries echo across the sand.
Then I made out a remarkable sight...

It was not a temple set amidst the trees,
where a young priestess, in love with the flowers,
her body burning hot in evening hours,
half-opens her robe to the passing breeze;

but, disturbing island birds as we sailed by,
close to the island's coast, we clearly saw
a three-branched gibbet set upon the shore,
standing out, cypress black, against the sky.

A ripe corpse dangled from it in the sun;
ferocious birds were perched on it, stabbing
into its bleeding corners with jabbing
and cruel beaks, destroying that rotting man.

Both eyes were holes; from the stomach's ruin
heavy intestines dangled to his thighs;
his torturers, gorged on delicacies,
had, with their beaks, fully castrated him.

And at his feet, a pack of hungry dogs,
squabbled and snarled and growled, their muzzles red;
one larger beast pushed through them, unhurried,
an executioner ringed by hired thugs.

Cytherean native, born in rich delights,
you have silently suffered these insults
for all the crimes and sins of your old cults,
barring you from proper burial rites.

Ridiculous hanged man, your pains are mine!
As I stared at your sorry fleshless form,
I felt my gall twist and rise like a worm
towards my mouth, tasting of putrid wine.

Poor devil, with your memory still fresh,
I too have felt the cutting beaks and jaws
of carrion crows and of black panthers,
who once so loved to feast upon my flesh.

– How beautiful the sky? How smooth the sea? –
For me, everything stays under black clouds,
and I, as though wrapped in a bloodied shroud,
have my heart buried in this allegory.

There's nothing standing on your isle, Venus,
but a gibbet and my own hanged image.
– Master! Give me the strength and the courage
to see my heart and body without disgust!

Love and the Skull

An old engraving

Love sits on the skull of
humanity,
and once upon this throne,
laughs profanely,

and gaily blows bubbles
that try to rise,
to rejoin the lost worlds
deep in the sky.

In perfect flight, the frail,
luminous globe
bursts apart its thin soul;
a dream of gold.

The skull, to each bubble,
begs and contends:
– "This vile, ferocious game,
when does it end?

What your mouth blows away,
like pouring rain,
murderer, is my flesh,
my blood and brain!"

REVOLT

Saint Peter's Renunciation

What does God make of all the heresies,
rising all day to his Seraphic throne?
Like a tyrant gorged on good meat and wine,
he sleeps through the sound of our blasphemies.

The sobs of martyrs and of the tortured
are a heady symphony, without doubt,
since, despite the cost of blood for their delight,
Heaven is not yet fully satisfied!

– Jesus, remember the Garden of Olives!
where you prayed on your knees, so free of guile,
to the ones who laughed at the sound of the nails
torturers planted in your flesh that lived.

When you saw them spit on your divinity,
the crude bodyguards and the servant scum,
and when you felt the thorns enter your skull,
the home of your immense humanity;

when your broken body's terrible weight
dragged on your dislocated arms, when your
blood and your sweat flowed down your paling brow;
when you were hung up there, like a target,

did you dream of those brilliant and calm hours,
when you went out to fulfil the true Word,
when, mounted on a kind she-ass, you trod
the paths all strewn with palm leaves and flowers;

when, your heart swollen with hope and lack of fear,
you whipped the merchants with all of your force,
when you were at last master, did remorse
pierce your side far deeper than any spear?

– Certainly, I'm glad to leave, for my part,
a world where acts and dreams are hollow words;
I'll live by –and perish by – my own sword!
Saint Peter denied Jesus... he was right!

Abel and Cain

1

Race of Abel, eat, drink and sleep;
God smiles on you complacently.

Race of Cain, in the mud you creep,
crawl and die in your misery.

Race of Abel, your sacrifice
smells sweet to all the holy choir!

Race of Cain, your torment and vice,
when will it ever be over?

Race of Abel, your new seeds grow;
and your crops prosper, strong and sound;

Race of Cain, your entrails now howl
with the hunger of an old hound.

Race of Abel, warm your bones
at your family's fire-side hearth;

Race of Cain, in your cave, alone
tremble with cold, jackal from birth!

Race of Abel, love, prosper, learn;
your gold has also multiplied.

Race of Cain, with a heart that burns,
beware of your great appetites.

Race of Abel, you feed and grow
as the wood beetles in the tree!

Race of Cain, along the long roads
you drag your accursed family.

2

Ah! Race of Abel, carrion,
you'll fertilize the smoking earth!

Race of Cain, your worthless work
is not supposed to be usurped;

Race of Abel, your shame won't end:
the sword is beaten by the rod!

Race of Cain, to heaven ascend,
and onto the Earth throw down God!

The Litanies of Satan

O you, most beautiful of Angels, wise,
you are betrayed – you are deprived of praise,

Satan, have pity on my misery!

Exile's ruler, each day you're defeated,
but you return stronger, still unbeaten,

Satan, have pity on my misery!

You know all things, you know the dark unknown,
familiar healer of human pain,

Satan, have pity on my misery!

You show them all – ill, outcast or despised,
the signs of a pure love in Paradise,

Satan, have pity on my misery!

You, along with your constant lover, death,
encourage hope – entwined with its madness!

Satan, have pity on my misery!

You give all of the condemned the clear calm
to damn the entire nations who would harm.

Satan, have pity on my misery!

On this envious Earth, you know the zones
in which the jealous hide the precious stones,

Satan, have pity on my misery!

You also know just where the fullest veins
of rare, valuable metals are enseamed,

Satan, have pity on my misery!

Your enormous hand hides the sudden edge
from the sleep-walker wandering the ledge,

Satan, have pity on my misery!

You somehow save the drunkard's poor old bones
from the dangers of staggering home, alone,

Satan, have pity on my misery!

You console the weak, who always suffer,
by teaching them methods to hurt others,

Satan, have pity on my misery!

You subtly place your mark on every sign:
Named, Labelled, Logoed, Trademarked, Advertised

Satan, have pity on my misery!

You, inside every girl's heart, have sustained
a love of rags, a cult of wounded pain,

Satan, have pity on my misery!

You endorse invention; promote all arts,
and hear the talk of executioners,

Satan, have pity on my misery!

You adopt everyone who is expelled
from paradise, by God, into a hell,

Satan, have pity on my misery!

Prayer

Glory and praise to you, Satan, on high,
where you once ruled; in deepest hell you lie,

133

defeated, where you dream your silent dreams!
Grant my soul be with you, beneath the tree
of knowledge, on that day, above your head,
when, like a new temple, its branches spread!

DEATH

The Death of Lovers

Our bed will be full of every perfume,
as will this deep divan, on which we lie,
and upon shelves, the rarest flowers will bloom
only for us, beneath a perfect sky.

Our hearts will be like two giant torches,
fighting to be the last one with the heat,
reflecting in our spirits' twin mirrors,
the doubled and repeated lights of each.

Then, on a rose and mystic blue evening,
we will exchange a flash of lightning,
like a long sob, all full of sad adieus;

later, an angel, opening all the doors,
will, faithful and joyful, rejuvenate
our mirrors and our fires that have burned-out.

The Death of the Poor

It's death that consoles us and makes us live;
it is the aim of life – our only hope,
that lifts us, gives us life and heart enough
to walk, restored, until the day's dark close;

through the storm, through the snow, and through the frost,
it's the clear light on a black horizon;
the famous inn written of in the books,
where we can sit and eat, and rest in calm;

it's an angel with great powers in its hands,
creating sleep and wild, ecstatic dreams;
making beds for the naked and the poor;

it's the glory of the gods, their attic rooms;
the poor man's purse and his antique homeland;
it's an unknown sky behind an ornate door.

The Death of Artists

How often do I have to ring my bells
and kiss your forehead, dull caricature?
How many times, quiver, must I fire bolts,
to hit that target – mystical nature?

Subtle strategies will wear out our souls
and destroy our heavy suits of armour,
long before we see the immense idol
and sob sadly at its depraved desires.

There are many who've never known icons,
and there are sculptors marked out by disgrace,
who hammer hard at their own breast and face,

with just one hope – strange, sombre and unkind;
the hope that death, that hovering black sun,
finds ways to open the flower of their mind.

The Journey's End

Beneath the pale sunlight, life runs,
dances and twists without reason,
yelling aloud and impudent.
And when above the horizon

the voluptuous night rises,
soothing everything, hunger too,
effacing all, even deep shame –
then the poet says aloud: "Now!

My spirit, like my tired spine screams
for some much-needed rest, repose,
with a heart full of gloomy dreams,

on my back I shall throw myself
and roll my body up inside
your curtains, refreshing darkness!"

The Dream of a Curious Man

To Félix Nadar

Do you, like me, know suffering's flavour?
Do you make others say, "That man is strange!"
– I was near dead. In my amorous soul
desire and horror mixed, an illness ranged;

anguish and hope merged without argument.
The more the clock ticks of the fatal hours,
the more my torture tastes of joy and hurt;
my heart is freed from the familiar.

Finally the brutal truth was revealed:
I had died. And now the terrible dawn
was enveloping me. – What! Was this all?

Like a child needing to see, and hating
the curtain as one hates all obstacles...
the curtain was up and I was still waiting.

The Voyage

To Maxime du Camp

1

For the child with a love of maps and stamps,
the world is equal to his appetite.
How vast the world is when lit up by lamps!
How small it is when held in memory's sight.

One morning we set sail, our minds on fire,
our resentful hearts full of hostility,
and followed the rhythms the waves inspired –
the infinite upon a finite sea;

some of us had left behind hated homes,
some were running from traumas of childhood,
some left their families so they could roam,
because their lives contained no earthly good.

To stay men, not beasts, they drink deep and long
of space and light and flaming, blazing skies;
they strengthen in the cold, tan in the strong
sunlight, forgetting their lusts and their lies.

But the true voyagers are those who go
so they can get there – their hearts light
and in tune with destiny; those who know
without knowing why, to say, "Yes" to flight;

those whose desires are shaped like clouds,
who always dream, as beginners dream of fame,
of pleasure, ever-changing, unknown, proud,
which human nature cannot give a name!

2

When we're awake, we dance out of control,
asleep, we imitate automatons,
curiosity torments us – it rolls
out, like a cruel angel, whipping the sun.

Strange fate – ever-changing goal, moving posts;
being nowhere it can be anywhere,
but mankind's hopes are never truly lost;
each day we race, convinced a heaven's there.

Our soul's a ship looking for our island;
"Look out!" a lone voice cries out, full of shock,
while other voices, crazy, ardent, sound:
"Love... Fame... Delight!" but it's a rock!

Each island sighted by the lookout seems
a Utopia promised by true fate;
imagination plans orgies and dreams,
then sees just rock by morning's clearest light.

What to do with the one who cries and raves
he's seen the promised land? – The fool insists
on paradise! Let's throw him in the waves,
he makes drowning more bitter than it is.

The tramp, shuffling at night through our slums,
finds with drunken eyes, islands of beauty

as he trudges past warm and bright-lit homes;
to him, they're all Mauritius or Capri.

3

Exotic travellers! What histories
are to be found in your deep sea-green eyes?
Show us films, your treasured memories,
those perfect jewels, those stars in their own skies.

We too would voyage – without wings or sails,
to break this ennui of our life's prisons,
so pass into our spirits all details;
let your memories fill our horizons.

Tell us, what have you seen?

4

"We've seen the stars
and some waves too, and quite a bit of sand,
and, despite the odd shock and disaster,
we were as bored there as in any land.

The light of the sun on the violet sea,
a distant city's outline at sunset,
made our hearts grow restless – we had to see
the worlds the skies alluringly reflect.

Not one city, not one single landscape,
contained the appeal or the mystery
of those vast billowing cloud shapes –
all we had were days of anxiety.

– We've found fulfilment increases desire
and desire's an old tree whose branches spread
towards the sun, stretching out further, higher,
absorbing the sun's warmth, and pleasure-fed,

always growing – greater than the cypress.
Anyway, people, dreamers, stay-at-homes,
we've brought you some footage of our travels;
we know you need to vicariously roam.

We've worshipped an elephant-headed god;
seen thrones built of gold constellations,
in palaces rich enough to provide
a merchant banker with palpitations;

clothes cut from cloth far too costly to wear;
women with tattooed skin and painted teeth,
magicians who could make great snakes appear."

5

And then! And then! What else?

6

"Oh children, please!

Oh yes, we ought to mention this one thing
we learned and sadly have not forgotten.
Wherever we went we saw in everything
the taint of human folly – of real sin:

Tyrant men, greedy, cruel and stupid,
always lazy and only moved by lust;
women, enslaved to louts, seeking cupid
in everything – loving without disgust;

martyrs wanting mercy, sadists who joke;
the festival season, the scent of blood;
the poison that enervates the despot,
and those who love the whip because they should;

so many religions – all like our own;
ladders to heaven, Saints who reign
over sanctity, and pleasurably moan
as they find paradise on beds of nails;

awed by its genius, humanity,
as insane as it's always going to be,
cries to god in tormented agony:
'My master, how I hate you. You are me.'

The least mad choose senility; others
round themselves up, letting fate lock their doors,
dulling lives with an opiate, no bother
to anyone. That's it for our report."

7

Sharp truths are at the end of a voyage:
the world is tedious and small – do we
see ourselves today, tomorrow, now, always,
as poisoned wells in deserts of ennui!

Should we stay? Go? Go if you must, or stay –
whichever you prefer – no one will care.
Time has his gloomy eye on us today,
and no one can escape his glassy stare.

For some: the Apostles, the Wandering Jew,
nowhere is right; there is no place on Earth
to avoid the nets flung out – one or two,
by dying at birth, manage to slip through.

When finally the foot stamps on our spine,
we'll still be hoping, crying as before –
as when we set off in that other time,
hair blown by the wind, eyes fixed on a star.

We set off over a sea of darkness,
with a young navigator's joyful heart;
can you hear those charming, but sad voices,
singing: "Come here, those of you who would eat

the perfumed Lotus flower. It is right here.
The fruit you hunger for is all you thought –
it's tender and it's strange, but never fear...
to taste it will bring you endless delight."

The voice is familiar – we know the ghosts –
dead sisters and companions of the past
hold out their arms in welcome: "Why be lost?
Come here with us and let your childhood last.

8

Well, Captain Death, it's time. Lift the anchor!
This country's dead; we've had enough. Let's go!
Let sky and sea be as dark as ichor;
our heart is full of light, as well you know.

We've drunk the poison, now we wish you well.
Fire burns in our minds – all now left to do
is dive through the depths of heaven or hell,
and on through the unknown to find the new.

ADDITIONAL POEMS

Pagan's Prayer

Ah! Do not extinguish your vibrant flames;
use them to warm my numbed and frozen heart,
Pleasure, you torturer of wretched souls!
Goddess! Please hear my ardent prayer to you!
Goddess – you permeate the very air
and flame brightly in underground caverns.
I dedicate this brazen hymn to you,
so grant this apathetic soul's request –
Pleasure, will you now be my pagan queen?
I crave that you put on a siren's mask
that's finely fashioned from flesh and velvet,
or pour me out a draught of your deep sleep
that is a formless and mystical wine,
Ah! Pleasure, elastic phantom – you're mine

The Abyss

Pascal had his abyss that followed him.
Everything is abyss: action, desire, dream – word.
I feel the wind of fear pass frequently
through my thick hair, which often stands on end,
up and down, everywhere, into the depths,
through silence, space, captivating, ugly...
During my nights, a god with clever hands
draws never-ending multi-shaped nightmares
and I'm afraid of sleep – it's a big hole
full of horrors that lead to the unknown.
Windows show me infinity. Seeing
it, my hurt mind suffers from vertigo.
How I envy the sense of nothingness;
I'm never free of numbers or of beings.

The Voice

My cot was in the library – a dark Babel
where everything mingled – novels, facts,

Roman histories: ash; Greek fables: dust.
I was no taller than a new hardback.

Two voices spoke. One was insidious.
It said: "The Earth's the fullest, sweetest cake;
I'll give you an appetite the same size;
endless pleasure is there for you to take."

The other voice said: "Travel in your dreams
beyond the possible, beyond the seen!"
And it sang like the wind along the shore,
a wailing ghost, that comes from who knows where,

kisses the ear and yet somehow still scares.
I answered: "Yes, sweet voice," and from that date
I could never name my sorrow or my fate.
Behind the huge scenery of this life,

in the immense darkness of the abyss,
I saw distinctly remarkable worlds.
But my visions did not cause me to be free,
for I trailed snakes that sank their fangs in me.

And since then, like all prophets, I think fondly
of the scorching desert and the wide sea.
I laugh at death; cry pointlessly for hours
and always find the sweetest wine tastes sour.

I take facts to be lies, or so it seems;
look up at heaven and too often fall,
but that consoling voice says: "Guard your dreams;
the wise envy the beautiful dreams of fools."

The Unforeseen

Harpagon, caring for his dying father,
looked at those white lips and thoughtfully said:
"It seems to me we have sufficient
old boards in the attic for when he's dead."

Célimène cooed and said: "My heart is good,
and of course God has made me beautiful."

147

Her heart was shrivelled, like an old smoked ham,
roasted in a flame that was eternal.

A smoking hack – a beacon to the world,
to readers he has drowned in darkness, says:
"Where then is this creator of beauty,
this paragon that you constantly praise?"

But best of all, I know a sensualist
who yawns night and day and laments and cries:
(the impotent fool): "Yes, all I desire
is to be virtuous for an hour!" He lies.

The clock whispers: "He is at last ready,
the damned one. Be warned, his flesh stinks,
he's blind and deaf, and is as unsteady
as a wall undermined by termites."

Then one appeared whom they had all denied,
who laughed mockingly, saying: "Friends, alas,
you've drunk from my chamber-pot many times,
and communed joyously at my Black Mass.

You've each built temples to me in your hearts;
kissed my buttocks – in secret you took part.
Know me as Satan by my conquering mirth,
as huge and ugly as the entire earth.

Surprised hypocrites, did you really think
you could cheat your teacher of what was his;
that you would naturally be given
two rewards: made rich and sent to heaven?

The hunter who stands shivering gets paid
for the long hours spent looking for his prey.
I'm going to take you all through the thickness;
you'll join me in my gloomy joy today.

Through the thickness of the earth and the rock,
through heaps of ashes that are piled in cones,
to a palace huge as I – a single block,
but one that's not made out of softest stone.

For it is made of Universal Sin,
and contains my pride, sorrow and glory!"
And perched on the top of the universe,
an Angel gives the sounds of victory

to those whose hearts say: "Blessed is your whip,
Lord! Father, let my suffering be blessed!
In your hands my soul's not an empty toy;
with your infinite knowledge, you know best."

The sound of the trumpet is delightful,
on heaven's most solemn harvest evening;
it ecstatically permeates anyone
who loves and praises what the trumpet sings.

Midnight Scrutiny

The clock stridently strikes midnight.
Its wound-down sound ironically
invites us to think of the use
that we've made of the working day.

Today it was a fateful date,
it was a Friday – the thirteenth,
and despite everything we know,
we've lived life as a heretic.

Today we have blasphemed Jesus,
the one God we cannot deny.
We're at the table – parasites
to some monstrous Croesus.

We have to please the beast in us;
the Devil's worthy advocate,
insulting everything we love,
and flattering all we should hate.

We have saddened the servile man,
the weak we've wrongfully despised.
we stupidly worshipped folly;
between the bull's horns it resides.

We have kissed all stupid matter;
kissed it with perfect devotion,
and we have bathed in the pale light
of our blessed putrefaction.

Finally, we've had to drown
vertigo in delirium.
We the are proud priests of the Lyre,
whose only glory is to show

the rapture of sorrowful things.
Drink – no thirst; feed – no appetite.
Quickly let us switch off the lamp,
and hide in the darkness of night.

Epigraph for a Condemned Book

Good person, sober and naïve;
reader of peaceful bucolics,
throw away this saturnine book,
orgiastic and melancholic.

Unless you've studied rhetoric
and mastered it in Satan's school,
abandon it – you understand –
or am I an hysterical fool?

But if, without being bewitched,
your eyes can withstand the abyss,
read me, love me and stay true.

Inquiring sufferer, you seek
paradise. So to you I speak:
pity me... or else I'll curse you!

ARTIFICIAL PARADISE

ON WINE AND HASHISH

1.

Wine

A very famous man, who was at the same time a great fool (things which, it would seem, go very well together, as I will undoubtedly more than once have the dubious pleasure of showing), had the effrontery to enter the following under the heading *Wine* in a book on Foods, written from the double point of view of Health and Taste:"Noah the Patriarch is considered to be the inventor of wine; it is an alcoholic beverage made of the fruit of the vine."

And then? Then, nothing: that is all. In vain you will leaf through the volume, turning it about in all directions, reading it backwards, inside out, from right to left and from left to right; you will find nothing more about wine in La Physiologie du Gout by the most illustrious, most highly respected Brillat-Savarin. "Noah the Patriarch..." and "it is an alcoholic beverage..."

I am picturing a moon man, or an inhabitant of some distant planet, travelling in our world; tired with his long trek, he seeks to cool his palate and warm his stomach. He is eager to acquaint himself with the delights and customs of our land. He has heard sketchy accounts of delicious beverages with which the citizens of this planet can at will secure courage and cheerfulness for themselves. So that he may be more sure of his choice, the moon man turns to that oracle of taste, the celebrated and infallible Brillat-Savarin, and there, under the heading *Wine,* he finds this gem of information: "Noah the Patriarch..." and "it is an alcoholic beverage..." *That* is quite a digestive. *That* is most explanatory. It is impossible, after reading that sentence, not to have a clear and precise idea of all the wines, of their different qualities, their drawbacks, their power over mind and stomach.

Ah! dear friends, don't read Brillat-Savarin. "God protects the ones He loves from worthless reading"; that is the first maxim in a little book by Lavater, a philosopher who loved mankind more than did all the magistrates of the Ancient and Modern Worlds. No cake has been named in Lavater's honor; but the memory of this angelic man will live on among Christians when even the worthy bourgeois have forgotten the Brillat-Savarin, that tasteless variety of roll, the least of whose defects is that it serves as a pretext for a twittering of foolishly pedantic maxims drawn from the famous chef-d'oeuvre.

You melancholy drinkers, you merry drinkers, you forgotten and ignored drinkers, all of you who seek in wine either remembrance or forgetfulness, and who, never finding either complete enough to suit you, no longer lift your eyes to heaven except through the bottom of the bottle: if a new edition of this mock masterpiece were to risk insulting modern humanity, would you buy a copy, and return good for evil, kindness for indifference?

I open the divine Hoffmann's *Kreisleriana,* and there I read a curious recommendation. The conscientious musician should avail himself of champagne to compose a comic opera. In it he will find the light and frothy gaiety called for by the genre. Religious music requires Rhine wine or Jurancon. In these there is the same intoxicating sorrow that underlies profound thoughts. On the other hand, Burgundy is indispensable to heroic music. It has all the intense passion and ardor of patriotism. There we certainly have a better approach to the question, and beyond the impassioned sentiment of a drinking man, I find in it an impartiality that does the greatest honor to a German.

Hoff mann had set up a unique psychological barometer designed to show him the various temperatures and atmospheric conditions of his soul. On it we find such calibrations as these: "Slightly ironic frame of mind, tempered by indulgence; feeling of loneliness, accompanied by profound self-content; musical merriment, musical ecstasy, musical storm; sarcastic merry-making that is unbearable even to me; desire to step out of my Self, extreme objectivity, fusion of my Self with all of Nature." Needless to say, the calibrations of Hoffmann's mental barometer were set in order of their appearance, just as is the case with ordinary barometers. I feel that an obvious kinship exists between this psychic barometer and Hoffmann's explanation of the musical qualities of wines.

At the point that death came to claim him, Hoffmann was just beginning to make money. Fortune was smiling upon him. As was the case with our beloved Balzac, it was only towards the end that he saw the realization of his earliest hopes. At that time, editors who were competing for publication of his tales in their almanacs would try to get into his good graces by including a case of French wines with the money they sent.

II

Who has not known the profound joys of wine? Everyone who has ever had remorse to appease, a memory to evoke, a grief to drown, a castle in Spain to build – in short, *everyone* – has invoked the mysterious god hidden in the fibres of the vine. How great is the spectacle of the wine, lit by an inner sun! How real and ardent is the second youth that man sips out of it. But how dreadful, too, are its crushing pleasures, its debilitating charms. And yet, if truth be told, which of you judges, you legislators, you men of the world – you who are sweetened by happiness, and graced by fortune with virtue and good health – which of you would have the merciless courage to condemn the confirmed drinker?

Moreover, wine is not always that terrible wrestler, sure of its victory, and sworn to have neither pity nor mercy. Wine is like man: you never know how much you can both scorn and respect it, love and hate it; nor can you tell how many sublime works or monstrous crimes it is capable of. Let us not be crueller towards it than we are towards ourselves; let us treat it as our equal.

I sometimes seem to hear the wine; it speaks with its soul, in the spirit voice heard only by spirits, and says, "Man, my beloved creature, even through my prison of glass and bolts of cork, I want to send you a song filled with good-fellowship, a song of joy and light and hope. I am not ungrateful; I know that I owe my life to you. I know how much you have labored, with the hot sun on your shoulders. You have given me life, and I will repay you. I will pay my debt liberally; for I feel an extraordinary joy when I tumble down a gullet dried by work. An honest man's chest is a dwelling far more pleasant than these cheerless and unfeeling wine-vaults. It is a joyful tomb, where I fulfill my destiny with enthusiasm. I raise a great hullabaloo in the working man's stomach; from there, I rise by invisible stairways to his brain, where I do my last great dance.

"Do you hear the powerful refrains of olden days, the songs of love and glory, rumbling and resounding in me? I am the soul of the Nation, half gallantry, half military might. I am Sunday's hope. Work enriches the weekdays, wine brings happiness to Sunday. Sitting with your elbows on the family table, your shirt-sleeves rolled up, you will do me proud honor; and you will feel truly content.

"I will light the eyes of your old wife, the aged companion of your daily trials and life-long hopes. I will soften her look, and put the gleam of youth back in her eye. And as for your beloved little son (how pale he is, poor little donkey, yoked like a workhorse in hard labor!), I will return the beautiful color of his infancy; for this new athlete of Life I will be like the oil that strengthened the muscles of wrestlers of old.

"I will tumble to the depths of your chest like ambrosia. I will be the seed that fertilizes the furrows you have toiled to plow. Our intimate union will create poetry. Together we two will become a god, and we will fly to infinity like the birds, and butterflies, and gossamer, and perfumes, and all winged things."

This is what the wine sings in its mysterious language. Worse luck to anyone whose selfish heart is so closed to the suffering of his brothers that he has never heard this song!

I have often thought that if Jesus Christ were to appear today in the dock of the accused, there would be some attorney who would show that the case against him was strengthened by the recurrence of his offenses. As for wine, its feats recur every day. Every day it repeats its kindnesses. Doubtless that accounts for the animosity that the moralists display towards it. When I say "moralists," I mean pseudo-moralistic hypocrites.

But that is something else again. Let us come down a bit lower. Let us look in on one of those mysterious creatures who live, as it were, on the waste matter of great cities; for there are indeed strange callings. Their number is immense. I have sometimes thought with terror that there are trades that bring no joy, trades without pleasure, heavy labors without relief, pains without compensation. I was wrong. Here we have a man whose job it is to pick up the day's rubbish in the capital. He collects and catalogues everything that the great city has cast off, everything it has lost, and discarded, and broken. He goes through the archives of debauchery, and the confused array of refuse. He makes a selection, an intelligent choice; like a miser hoarding treasure, he collects the garbage that will become objects of utility or pleasure when refurbished by Industrial magic. Here he is, in the grim flickering light of street-lamps blown by the night wind, as he goes back up Saint-Genevieve Hill, along one of the long, winding streets inhabited by a large number of little families. He is wearing his wicker shoulder basket, with its pike attached. He comes up, shaking his head and stumbling over the paving stones, like the young poets who spend their days wandering about in search of rhymes. He is talking to himself; he is pouring his soul out in the cold, dark air of the night. It's a monologue splendid enough to make the most lyric tragedies seem pitiful. "Forward, march! Company, about face!" Just like Bonaparte, dying on Saint Helena!

His pike seems to have changed into an iron scepter, and the wicker basket has become an imperial robe. Now he is complimenting his army. The battle has been won, but the day was hot. He is riding on horseback beneath triumphal arches. His heart is happy. With pleasure he hears the acclamation of an enthusiastic world. Presently he will impose a law better than any law ever known. He solemnly swears that he will make his people happy. Poverty and vice have disappeared from humanity.

And yet, his back and loins have been skinned bare by the weight of his basket. He is harried by family problems. He has been bruised by forty years of work and running about. His age causes him to suffer. But wine, like the river Pactolus of yore, rolls an intellectual gold through languishing humanity. Like a good king, it reigns by serving, and sings its grand deeds through its subjects' throats.

On this terrestrial globe there is a numberless, nameless crowd whose pain could never be sufficiently anaesthetized by sleep. Wine composes songs and poems for them.

Many people will undoubtedly find me very indulgent. "You are excusing chronic insobriety, you are idealizing drunkenness." I admit that in the face of the benefits I do not have the heart to count the wrongs. Furthermore, I have said that wine was similar to man, and I have granted that their crimes were equal to their virtues. Can I do more? Besides, I have another theory. If wine were to disappear from production on earth, I believe that it would leave a void, an absence, an imperfection in the health and mentality of the planet; and this would be far more frightful than all the surfeits, all the deviations, for which we hold wine responsible. Whether they do so out of naïveté or by specific design, is it unreasonable to think that people who refrain from ever drinking wine are either imbeciles or hypocrites? When I say imbeciles, I mean men who know neither humanity nor nature; artists who reject the traditional artistic methods; mechanics who curse machinery. By hypocrites, I mean gluttons who are ashamed of themselves; braggarts who vaunt their sobriety, but in secret drink the wines they keep hidden about the house. A man who drinks only water has a secret to hide from his fellow men.

Let us consider the question: several years ago, at an art exhibition, a pack of imbeciles created an uproar in front of a picture that was polished, waxed, and varnished like some industrial product. It was the absolute antithesis of art; it was to Drolling's *Kitchen* what folly is to foolishness, and what blind devotion is to imitation. This microscopic painting showed flies flitting about. Like everyone else, I was drawn towards the monstrous thing; but I was ashamed of this singular weakness, representing as it did the irresistible attraction in horrible things. In the end, I realized that I had been drawn along, without quite knowing it, by a philosophical curiosity – an immense desire to know what kind of moral character belonged to the man who had fathered such criminal eccentricity. I wagered myself that he must be fundamentally evil. I had inquiries made, and my instincts were gratified by winning this psychological bet. I learned that the monster arose regularly before dawn; that he had brought his charwoman to ruin; and that *he drank only milk!*

One or two more stories, and we will take a stand. One day, I saw a great throng on the sidewalk. I managed to get a look over the shoulders of some of the voyeurs, and this is what I saw: a man was lying flat on his back upon the ground, his eyes open, staring at the sky. Standing before him was another man, who was conversing with him through gestures, to which the fellow on the ground replied only with his eyes. Both seemed to be animated by stupendous good will. The gestures of the standing man were saying to the mind of the fellow on the ground, "Come on, just a little bit farther, happiness is there, two steps away, come on to the corner. We haven't quite lost sight of the shoreline of Sorrow; we're not yet out on the high seas of dream; come on, buck up, friend! Tell your legs to do your mind."

And all that was accompanied by much reeling and staggering. The other fellow had doubtless already reached the high seas (moreover, he was at full sail in the gutter), for his blissful smile replied, "Leave your old pal alone. The shoreline of Sorrow has disappeared well enough behind a merciful fog; I no longer ask anything in the way of dreams." I think that I even heard an indistinct sentence – or rather, a sigh, indistinctly shaped into words – escape his lips! "You have to know when to stop." This was the ultimate in sublimity. But in intoxication there is hypersublimity, as you will see. Still filled with indulgence, the friend went off alone to the tavern, then returned, holding a rope. No doubt he couldn't bear the idea of navigating alone, and alone pursuing happiness; that is why he came to pick up his friend in a conveyance. The conveyance was the rope; he slipped the conveyance about his hips. His friend, still flat on his back, was smiling: no doubt he understood this maternal sentiment. The other fellow tied a knot; then he fell into line, like a gentle and considerate horse, and carted his friend to their rendez-vous with Happiness. The fellow who was being carted – or rather, dragged – and who was polishing the pavement with his back, continued to smile an indescribable smile.

The crowd was stunned; for anything that is too beautiful, anything that goes beyond man's poetic skill, produces more astonishment than tenderness.

There was a Spanish fellow, a guitarist, who for some time travelled with Paganini: this was before the time of Paganini's great official prestige.

They both led the great vagabond life of bohemians and travelling musicians, people without national or family ties. Together, violin and guitar gave concerts everywhere they went. For a long while they wandered about like this through various countries. My Spaniard had such talent that, like Orpheus, he could say, "I am the ruler of nature."

Everywhere he went, strumming his strings, and making them leap melodically beneath his thumb, he was sure to be followed by a crowd. With a secret like that, no one ever starves. They followed him just as once they had followed Jesus Christ. How could you refuse dinner and hospitality to the man – the genius, the *sorcerer* – who made his most beautiful tunes, his most secret and unknown and mysterious melodies, sing to your soul? I have been assured that the fellow easily obtained continuous sound on an instrument that only produces separate, consecutive sounds. Paganini kept the money; he was in charge of their capital, which will surprise no one.

The cash was always on the manager's person; now it was upstairs, now downstairs; today it was in his boots, tomorrow it would be in the lining of his suit. Whenever the guitarist, a heavy drinker, asked what their financial situation was, Paganini would answer that there was nothing left, or at least almost nothing; for Paganini was like the old people, afraid of being *in need*. The Spaniard would believe him, or pretend to believe him; and staring into the horizon, he would strum and fret his inseparable companion. Paganini always walked on the other side of the road. This was done by mutual agreement, so that they would not disturb one another. In this way, each one could study and work while walking.

Then, when they had reached a place that offered some chance of a good financial take, one of the pair would play one of his compositions, while the other would improvise a variation, a harmony, a counter-melody alongside him. No one will ever know how much joy and poetry there was in that troubadour existence. They parted company – I don't know why. The Spaniard travelled alone. One evening he arrived at a small city in the Jura; he had the word spread that there would be a concert in a room of the town hall. *He* would be the concert, alone with his guitar. He made himself known by strumming away in certain cafés; and there were a number of musicians in the city who were struck by his strange talent. In the end, a good crowd came.

In an obscure corner of the city, beside the cemetery, our Spaniard had unearthed another Spaniard, a native of his own village, no less. The latter was a kind of burial-stone dealer, a marble-cutter who fashioned tombs. Like everyone in the funeral trades, he drank a lot. So a taste for the bottle, and their common nationality, led them far; the musician simply would not leave the marble-cutter. On the very day of the concert, at the appointed hour, they were together – but where? That was what had to be found out. They scoured every tavern in the city, every café. Finally, they dug the musician up in an indescribable hole; both he and his friend were perfectly drunk. There ensued a scene worthy of a Kean or a Frederick; but in the end he consented to play. Suddenly, he was taken by an idea: "You will play with me," he said to his friend. The latter refused; he had a violin, but he was quite a dreadful fiddler. "Either you play, or I don't."

No warnings, no good reasons would prevail; he had to give in. There they were on the stage, before the refined bourgeoisie of the area. "Bring some wine," said the Spaniard. The tomb-stone maker, who was known by everyone, but hardly as a musician, was too drunk to be ashamed. When the wine had been brought, they no longer had the patience to uncork the bottles. The unsightly rogues guillotined them with jabs of a knife, like people who had been badly brought up. Consider what a fine effect this had on all the dressed-up country folk! The ladies withdrew, and many people, completely scandalized, fled before this pair of drunks who seemed half mad.

But it was well worth it to anyone whose sense of propriety had not extinguished his curiosity, anyone who had the courage to remain. "Begin," said the guitarist to the marble-cutter. It is impossible to describe the kind of sound that issued from the drunken violin; the sound of a delirious Bacchus cutting stone with a saw. What did he play, or try to play? It mattered little, after the first tune was heard. Suddenly, a melody at once soft, lively, whimsical, surrounded the noisy din, suppressing it, smothering it, concealing it. The guitar was singing so loud that the violin could no longer be heard. And yet it was indeed the tune, the very same wine-soaked tune that the marble-cutter had bitten into.

The guitar expressed itself with enormous resonance; it

babbled, it sang, it declaimed, with alarming spirit, and unheard-of sureness and purity of diction. The guitar was improvising a variation on the violin's theme. It was letting the theme guide it, while it garbed the slender nudity of its sound with splendor and a maternal tenderness. The reader will understand that such a scene is beyond description; a sincere and truthful witness told me of it. In the end, the public was more drunk than he. The Spaniard was feted, complimented, greeted with immense enthusiasm. But doubtless the character of the local people displeased him; for that was the only time that he ever consented to play.

And now where is he? What sun gazed down upon his final dreams? What soil received his cosmopolitan remains? What ditch gave shelter to his dying agony? Where are the intoxicating scents of vanished flowers? Where are the magic colors of dead sunsets?

III.

Undoubtedly, I have taught you nothing very new. Wine is known and loved by all. Someday, when there is a doctor of truly philosophical bent (a very rare animal, indeed), he will be able to conduct a powerful study on wine, a sort of double psychology, in which wine and man compose the two terms. He will explain how and why certain beverages have the ability to increase human individuality beyond all measure, and are able to create a sort of third person, by a mystical process wherein natural man and wine-the animal deity and the plant god-play the roles of Father and Son in the Trinity; together they engender a Holy Spirit, a kind of better man, who is the issue of both.

Some people are improved so markedly by wine that their legs grow steadier, and their hearing becomes more acute. I once knew a fellow whose weak eyesight was restored to its original keenness whenever he was drunk.

Long ago, an unknown author said, "Nothing equals the joy of the drinking man, if not the joy of the wine on being drunk." Wine plays an intimate part in human life – so intimate, indeed, that I would not be at all surprised if some enlightened soul, attracted by the pantheistic concept, were to attribute a kind of personality to it. Wine and man appear to me as two friendly wrestling-mates, forever in combat, and ever reconciled. The vanquished always embraces the victor.

There are wicked drunkards; but these are men who are naturally wicked. Bad men become execrable, just as good men become excellent.

Presently, I will discuss a substance that has come into fashion in the past few years, a drug that delights a certain class of dilettantes, and produces effects far more powerful and crushing than those of wine. I will carefully describe all of its effects; then, resuming my description of the different effects of wine, I will compare these two artificial methods whereby man can stoke the fires of his individuality, and create a sort of divinity within himself.

I will indicate the drawbacks of hashish, the least of which (despite the wealth of benevolence that it seems to cultivate in the heart – or rather, the brain – of man), the very least of which, I repeat, is that it is "antisocial," while wine is profoundly human; I would even venture to call it a "man of action."

IV.

Hashish

When the hemp is harvested, strange phenomena sometimes occur among both male and female workers. It would seem as if some undefinable, dizzying spirit were emerging from the harvest to flow about their legs and rise maliciously to their brains. The reaper's head spins in a vortex; at other times, he is disturbed by dreams. His limbs grow weak, and will not serve him. Furthermore, similar things happened to me when, as a child, I used to play and roll about in piles of alfalfa.

Attempts were made to produce hashish with French hemp. Every attempt to date has failed, and the desperate fiends who will avail themselves of mystical pleasures at any price have continued to use hashish from across the Mediterranean – that is, hashish made with Indian or Egyptian hemp. Hashish is composed of a decoction of Indian hemp, butter, and a small quantity of opium.

Here we have a strange-smelling green jelly, with an odor that arouses a certain repulsion, as, moreover, would any subtle odor brought to its maximum force and density, so to speak. Take a drop, just a teaspoonful, and happiness is yours: total happiness with all its intoxication, all its childish folly, all its boundless bliss. Behold happiness, in the form of a bit of jelly; help yourself to it without fear – it won't kill you. Your bodily organs will be done no serious harm by it. Perhaps your strength of will may be diminished, but that is altogether another question.

If hashish is to have full strength and expansion, it is generally necessary to dilute it in very hot black coffee, and take it on an empty stomach. Dinner is postponed until ten o'clock or midnight; only a very light soup is permitted. Any infraction of this simple rule would either cause vomiting, when the drug disagreed with the dinner, or bring about the inefficacy of the hashish. Many fools and inexperienced people have acted thus, and charged the hashish with impotence.

No sooner has the drug been consumed (an operation which, moreover, demands a certain amount of resolve since, as I have said, the stuff smells so, that it causes a hint of nausea in some people) than you find yourself in a state of anxiety. You have already heard, in very sketchy terms, of the wonderful effects of hashish; your imagination has conceived a specific idea, an idealized intoxication, and now you are all eagerness to know whether, in reality, the results will come up to your anticipations. The time that elapses between consumption of the beverage and the onset of the first symptoms varies according to individual temperament and familiarity with the drug. People who are well versed in the ways of hashish sometimes feel the first symptoms after half an hour.

I have neglected to mention that since hashish causes an intensification of one's individuality, as well as a very keen awareness of events and settings, it would be best to resort to it only in favorable circumstances and surroundings. Whereas every joy and comfort is intensified, every grief or anguish becomes immensely profound. Don't experiment on your own with hashish if you have any unpleasant business to attend to, if your spirits are on the low side, or if you have a bill to pay. I have said that hashish is inadequate to stimulate positive action. It does not console you like wine; it only acts to expand a person's individuality beyond all measure, in relation to the circumstances that he happens to be in at the time. As far as possible, it is essential to locate yourself in a lovely apartment or a pretty countryside, and to have a free and unencumbered mind, and a few cohorts whose intellectual leanings are compatible with your own; a bit of music helps, too, if it is available.

More often than not, during their first experience, new users will complain of the delay in manifestation of the effects. They await them with anxiety, and when things don't happen quickly enough to suit them, they loudly vaunt their incredulity, which greatly amuses the experienced users who know how hashish operates. It is not without humor to see the first seizures appear and increase in the very midst of this incredulity. At first, a certain absurd, irresistible hilarity overcomes you. The most ordinary words, the simplest ideas assume a new and bizarre aspect. This mirth is intolerable to you; but it is useless to resist. The demon has invaded you; your every effort of resistance will serve only to accelerate the progress of the condition. You laugh at your own foolishness and nonsense; your companions laugh in your face, but you do not mind, because the characteristic good will is beginning to manifest itself.

The feeble gaiety, the uneasiness that you feel even in your joy, the failure of the intoxication to materialize fully, all are generally of short duration. It sometimes happens that people completely unsuited for word-play will improvise an endless string of puns and wholly improbable idea relationships fit to outdo the ablest masters of this preposterous craft. But after a few minutes, the relation between ideas becomes so vague, and the thread of your thoughts grows so tenuous, that only your cohorts, your co-religionists, can understand you. Your playfulness and bursts of laughter seem the ultimate in foolishness to anyone who is not in the same condition as you.

The propriety of those sober wretches delights you beyond all measure; their composure spurs you on to the final extremes of sarcasm; to you they appear the most foolish and ridiculous of men. As for your companions, you are perfectly attuned to them. Soon you are able to communicate with only a look. It is indeed a tolerably funny situation when a group of people are enjoying a joke that is incomprehensible to any outsider. They feel profound pity for the fellow who has been excluded. From this pity stems an idea of the superiority of their intellect. By and by, this idea will expand inordinately.

I have witnessed two rather grotesque scenes that took place during this first phase. A famous musician who knew nothing of the virtues of hashish – who perhaps had never even heard much talk of it – arrived at a gathering where almost everyone had taken the drug. Everyone tried to make him understand its wonderful effects. He laughed gracefully, like a man who is willing to go along with a thing for a few minutes in a spirit of decency, because he has been brought up well. There was much laughter, for people who have taken hashish are endowed with a marvellous sense of fun during the first stage. The bursts of laughter, the incomprehensible absurdities, the tangled strings of puns, the grotesque gestures all continued. The musician declared that this was a very bad artistic joke, which must, moreover, be quite exhausting for the participants.

The mirth increased. "This joke may seem good to you, but it doesn't to me," he said. "It's quite enough that it should seem good to *us*," one of the affected creatures selfishly replied. Endless whoops of laughter filled the room. Our man grew angry, and wanted to leave. Someone locked the door, and hid the key. Someone else got down on his knees before him, and weeping, swore to him, on behalf of the entire group, that even if they were moved with the deepest pity for him on account of his inferiority, they would nonetheless continue to find eternal kindness for him.

Everyone begged him for some music, and he gave in. Hardly had the violin been heard, when the notes that flowed through the apartment seemed to grip a few of the afflicted individuals who were lying about. There was nothing but deep sighs, sobs, heart-rending moans, and rivers of tears. The terrified musician stopped, thinking himself in a madhouse. He approached the fellow whose ecstatic condition was creating the loudest uproar, and asked him whether he was suffering much, and what would be necessary to relieve him. Some down-to-earth type, who hadn't touched the hashish either, suggested lemonade and sours. The hashish victim, the light of rapture in his eyes, flashed a look of unspeakable contempt at him: his pride was saving him from the gravest possible wrong. Indeed, what is more likely to exasperate a person sick with joy than to want to cure him?

Then, there is an event which I found extremely curious: a servant who had been entrusted to fetch tobacco and refreshments for a group of people under the influence of hashish, noticed that she was surrounded by weird, unnaturally wide-eyed faces. The unhealthy atmosphere, the mass insanity, seemed to leave her witless; she gave a crazy laugh, dropped her tray, shattering its load of cups and glasses; and charged in terror from the room at top speed. Everybody laughed. The following day, she confessed that for several hours she had felt something strange, had been "all funny and stuff." And yet, she hadn't actually taken hashish.

The second stage is ushered in by a sensation of coldness in the extremities, and a great over-all weakness. You are all thumbs, as they say; your head is heavy, and there is a general numbness throughout your being. Your eyes dilate; they seem drawn in every direction by an implacable ecstasy. Your face pales, and becomes a livid greenish color. Your lips narrow, contract, and seem to want to turn inward. Deep, hoarse sighs burst from your chest, as if the old "you" were unable to bear the weight of the new. Your senses become extraordinarily keen and acute. Your sight is infinite. Your ear can discern the slightest perceptible sound, even through the shrillest of noises.

Now the hallucinations begin. Outside objects assume monstrous appearance. They reveal themselves to you in new and unknown forms. They grow shapeless, reshape themselves, and end by becoming part of you; or rather, you become a part of them. The strangest ambiguities, the most inexplicable transpositions of ideas take place. In sounds there is color; in colors there is a music. Musical notes become numbers, and you solve stupendous arithmetical computations with alarming speed as the music reaches your ear. You are sitting and smoking; you believe that you are sitting in your pipe, and that *your pipe* is smoking *you*; you are exhaling *yourself* in bluish clouds.

You feel just fine in this position, and only one thing gives you worry or concern: how will you ever be able to get out of your pipe? This fantasy goes on for an eternity. A lucid interval, and a great expenditure of effort, permit you to look at the clock. The eternity turns out to have been only a minute. Another stream of ideas sweeps you away; it will carry you along for a moment in its rushing whirlpool; and this moment, too, will seem an eternity. One's sense of temporal and existential proportions is disturbed by the innumerable swarms of intense feelings and ideas. One lives several lifetimes in the space of an hour. This is precisely what is spoken of in *La Peau de Chagrin*. There is no longer any relationship between your body and the pleasure.

From time to time, your personality will vanish. The same objectivity that is the making of certain pantheistic poets and all the great comedians will work on you, so that your identity will blend with things outside yourself. Here you are, as a tree, moaning in the wind, whining plant melodies to nature... Now you are soaring through the immense blue expanses of the sky. Every trace of suffering is gone. You are no longer struggling; you have been borne aloft; no longer are you your own master, but this does not trouble you. By and by, your sense of time will vanish completely. Every once in a while you reawaken for a bit. You seem to be emerging from a wonderful, fantastic world. It is true that you are still capable of self-perception, and tomorrow you will remember some of your sensations. But you cannot apply this psychological ability. I defy you to sharpen a pencil; the effort involved would be beyond your capacity.

On other occasions, the music recites endless poems to you, setting you in frightening or enchanting dramas. It becomes associated with the things before your eyes. Ceiling frescoes, even bad or mediocre ones, come to life in the most startling manner. Water flows, clear and beguiling, through the trembling grass. Nymphs in radiant nudity look down at you, their large eyes clearer than water or sky. You would assume your position and your role in the naughtiest of paintings, the coarsest hangings plastering the walls of cheap hotels.

I have noticed that water assumes a terrible fascination for people of artistic inclination under the influence of hashish. Runnling water, fountains, melodious cascades: all are there, rolling, sleeping, singing, at the back of your mind. It would not do to leave a man in this condition beside clear water; like the fisherman of the ballad, he might let himself be carried off by the water-sprite.

Towards the end of the evening, it is possible to eat; but this is not done without some difficulty. You are so far above material concerns that you would certainly prefer to remain stretched out in the depths of your intellectual paradise. Sometimes, however, one's appetite grows in an extraordinary manner; still, it requires a great deal of courage to lift a bottle, a fork, and a knife.

The third phase, (separated from the second by a redoubled attack of dizzying intoxication, followed by further discomfort) is something beyond description. It is what the Orientals call *kief*; it is complete happiness. There is nothing whirling and tumultuous about it. It is a calm and placid beatitude. Every philosophical problem is resolved. Every difficult question that presents a point of contention for theologians, and brings despair to thoughtful men, becomes clear and transparent. Every contradiction is reconciled. Man has surpassed the gods.

Something within you says, "You are superior to all men; no one understands what you are thinking and feeling now. They are even incapable of understanding the immense love that you feel for them. But you should not hate them for that; you should pity them. A wealth of happiness and virtue is opening before you. No one will ever know the degree of virtue and intelligence that you have attained. Live in the solitude of your thoughts, and take care not to hurt anyone."

One of the oddest effects of hashish is a particular dread (sometimes carried to the point of insanity) of hurting anyone at all. If you had the strength, you would even disguise your extranatural condition, so as not to worry even the most insignificant of men.

Among tender and artistic people caught in this supreme condition, love assumes the strangest shapes, and lends itself to the most bizarre combinations. Unbridled wantonness may be mixed with a feeling of fervent paternal affection.

My final observation will not be the least curious. The following morning, when you see the daylight in your room, your first sensation is profound astonishment. Time has completely disappeared. A moment ago, it was night; now it is day. "Was I asleep, or wasn't I? Don't tell me that the intoxication went on all night, so that I lost all track of time, and the whole night hardly seemed a second to me! Or was I shrouded in the veils of a dream-laden sleep?" It is impossible to tell.

You seem to feel a well-being and a wonderful lightness of spirit: no fatigue. But hardly are you on your feet when a trace of the old intoxication appears. Your weak legs guide you timidly; you are afraid of breaking yourself like some fragile object. A great languor – not without a certain charm – grips your spirit. You are incapable of work or energetic action.

This is the just punishment for your ungodly waste of so

much nervous energy. You have strewn your personality in all directions, and now you are having a bit of difficulty in putting it back together again.

V.

I do not say that hashish produces all the effects that I have just described in *every* person. With the exception of a few variant forms, I have related nearly all the phenomena that generally occur in artistic and philosophical souls. But there are types in whom the drug displays only raucous foolery, an excessive mirth bordering on giddiness, and constant dancing, jumping, footstamping, and bursts of laughter. They have a very gross hashish "high", as it were. They are intolerable to the more spiritual types, who feel great pity for them. Their ugly personality glares out. I once saw a respectable magistrate, an honorable man (as society folk say of themselves), one of those people whose artificial decorum is always awe-inspiring; at the moment that hashish took possession of him, he suddenly began to jump about in the most indecent can-can imaginable. The true inner monster was revealing itself. This man who judged the actions of his peers, this *Togatus*, had secretly learned the can-can.

It may, then, be asserted that the impersonality, the objectivity to which I referred, is only the extreme unfolding of a poetic mind, and will never be found in the hashish of that other kind of person.

VI

In Egypt, the government forbids the sale and trafficking of hashish, at least inside the country. The wretched creatures who have a taste for it go to the pharmacist, under pretext of purchasing some other drug, and there receive the little dose that has been set aside for them. The Egyptian government is quite right. No enlightened state could ever subsist with the use of hashish; it builds neither warriors nor citizens. Indeed, under penalty of decadence and intellectual death, man is forbidden to disturb the primordial conditions of his existence, or break the equilibrium between his mind and the environment. If there were a government in whose interest it was to corrupt its subjects, the only thing necessary would be to encourage the use of hashish.

It is said that this substance causes no physical harm. That is true, or at least it has been considered so until now. But even if a man's body were in perfect condition, I do not know how long one could continue to say that he was in good health, if he could do nothing but dream, and were incapable of any positive action. For it is the Will that is attacked, and the Will is the body's most precious organ. If a man can instantly procure all wealth in heaven and earth by taking a teaspoonful of jelly, then he will never seek to acquire the slightest fraction of it by working. And our most urgent need is to live and work!

It occurred to me to treat wine and hashish in the same article, because they do indeed have something in common: both cause an inordinate poetic evolvement in men. Man's greatness is attested by his frantic craving for all things – healthful or otherwise – that excite his individuality. He seeks always to rekindle his hopes, and rise to infinity. But we must examine the results. On the one hand, we have a beverage that aids digestion, strengthens the muscles, and enriches the blood. Even when taken in large quantities, it causes only relatively short-lived disorders. On the other hand, we have a substance that disturbs the digestive processes, weakens the limbs, and is capable of producing an intoxication that lasts up to twenty-four hours. Wine exalts the Will, hashish destroys it. Wine is a physical support, hashish a suicidal weapon. Wine makes a man good-natured and sociable; hashish isolates him. The one is industrious, as it were; the other, essentially lazy. Indeed, what point is there in working, toiling, writing, creating anything at all, when it is possible to obtain Paradise in a single swallow? In a word, wine is for the working man, who deserves to drink of it. Hashish belongs to the class of solitary pleasures; it is made for the pitiful creatures with time on their hands. Wine is useful, it yields fruitful results. Hashish is useless and dangerous.[1]

It is only by way of reminder that I mention the recent attempt to apply hashish to the cure of madness. A madman who takes hashish contracts a new madness that puts the other to flight; but once the intoxication has run its course, true madness, which is the madman's norm, resumes dominion, just as health and reason do in us. Someone or other has actually taken the trouble to write a book about all this. The doctor who dreamed up this fine system is hardly what could be called a philosopher. —CB.

VII.

I conclude this article with a few apt words which are not my own, but which come from a remarkable, little-known philosopher, Barbereau, who is also a musical theorist and a professor at the Conservatory. I was with him at a gathering where several people had taken the blissful poison, and he remarked to me, in a tone of unspeakable contempt, "I just do not understand why rational and intelligent men use artificial means to attain poetic rapture, when enthusiasm and strength of will are enough to lift them to a supranatural level of existence. The great poets, the philosophers, the prophets, are all people who can succeed, simply by a free exertion of will, in reaching a state where they are at once cause and effect, subject and object, mesmerist and one entranced."

My own thoughts, exactly.

Get Drunk

(A Poem in Prose)

You must be drunk at all times. *That* is everything: the *only* question. If you would not feel the horrid weight of Time, that breaks your shoulders, bending you toward earth, relentlessly you must get drunk.

Well, then; but on what? On wine, or poetry, or virtue, as you will. Only, just get drunk!

And if, someday, you should awake upon a palace stair, or lying in the green grass of a ditch, or in the dreary loneness of your room, and you should find your drunkenness already lessened or quite gone, then ask of the wind, of the wave, of the star, of the lark, of the clock,-of all that flies, or rolls, or moans, or sings, or speaks-"What time is it?" And the wind, the wave, the star, the lark, the clock will answer, "It is time to get drunk! If you would not be the martyred slave of Time, get drunk, and never stop! On wine, or poetry, or virtue, as you will."

THE POEM OF HASHISH

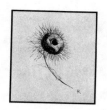

TO
J.G.F.

My dear friend,

Good sense tells us that the things of this earth barely exist at all, and true reality is to be found only in dreams. If one wishes to digest happiness – be it natural or artificial – one must first have the courage to swallow it; but somehow, those who seem to deserve happiness are precisely the ones for whom happiness, such as mortals conceive it, acts as a vomitive.

It will seem odd, even impertinent, to simple minds, that a survey of artificial pleasures should be dedicated to a woman, the commonest source of the most natural pleasures. Yet it is evident that since the natural world does penetrate into the world of the mind, providing it with fodder, and contributing to the operation of the indefinable amalgam that we call our individuality, it is woman that casts the darkest shadow or the brightest light into our dreams. Woman is inevitably suggestive; she lives by a life other than her own; she lives intellectually in the imaginations that she haunts and fires.

Furthermore, it little matters whether the reason for this dedication is understood. Is it even very necessary, for the author's satisfaction, that a given book be understood by anyone except the person for whom it was written? Is it, in the end, absolutely vital that it should have been written for someone? For my part, I have so little liking for the world of the living, that I would gladly write only for the dead, after the fashion of those sensitive ladies with little else to do, who are said to mail their confidences to imaginary friends.

But it is not to a dead person that I am dedicating this little book; rather, it is to someone who, though ailing, is alive and well in me; someone who now turns her eyes to Heaven, place of all transfigurations. For humankind enjoys the privilege of being able to extract constant acute pleasure from suffering, catastrophe and doom, as well as from powerful drugs.

In this tableau you will see a grave and solitary wanderer who, caught up in the moving tide of multitudes, sends his heart and thoughts to the far-off Electra who once wiped his sweat-bathed brow, and cooled his lips when they were parched with fever; and you will understand the gratitude of that other Orestes over whom you often remained wakeful, watching for nightmares, and from whom your soft, maternal hand chased the dreadful sleep.

C. B.

I.

The Taste for Infinity

People who know how to observe themselves and retain the
memory of their impressions, people who, like Hoffmann, have
been able to set up their mental barometers, from time to time have
had occasion to note lovely seasons, happy days, delicious minutes
in the observatory of their minds. There are days when a man will
awaken with a young and vigorous spirit. Hardly will his eyes be
cleared of the sleep that has sealed them, when the outside world
will present itself to him in striking relief, all clean contour and
wonderful rich color. The intellectual world opens its vast
perspectives, filled with new enlightenments. A man favored by
such regrettably rare and fleeting beatitude will feel at once more
artistic and more righteous-in a word, more noble. But the strangest
part of this exceptional mental and sensual state (which may,
without exaggeration, be called paradisiac, when compared with
the oppressive gloom of ordinary day-to-day existence,) is that it
was not brought on by any easily defined visible cause. Is it the
result of good health habits and a sensible diet? That is the first
explanation that comes to mind; but we are forced to acknowledge
that often this marvel, this wonder, occurs as if it were the doing of
some superior and invisible extra-human power, following a period
when a person has been abusing his physical resources. Should we
say that it is a reward for assiduous prayer and spiritual ardor?
Certainly, a constant uplifting of one's aspirations, a striving of one's
spirtual forces towards heaven, would be the ideal regimen to
create such glorious, radiant mental health; but, then, by what
absurd law does it sometimes appear following sinful orgies of the
imagination, or after a sophistical abuse of reason, as alien to its
proper, rational use as feats of contortion are to good, wholesome
gymnastics? That is why I prefer to consider this abnormal mental
condition as a true state of grace, or as a magic mirror where man
is invited to behold himself in beauty, which is to say, as he *could*
and *should* be; it is a sort of angelic excitation, a call to order in a
most complimentary form. Similarly, a centam Spiritualist school,
established in England and America, considers supernatural
phenomena such as the appearance of phantoms, ghosts, and so

forth, as manifestations of divine will, seeking to reawaken memory of invisible realities in the mind of man.

Furthermore, there are no symptoms that foretell the advent of this strange and delightful condition, in which all one's forces are in perfect balance, and one's imagination, wonderfully powerful though it may be, does not drag one's moral sense along behind it, on perilous escapades. The delicate sensitivity that one possesses is no longer strained by sick nerves, the usual counsel of crime and despair. This wonderful condition, I repeat, is as unforeseen as the phantom. It is a sort of visitation, but an *intermittent* one, from which, if we were wise, we would be bound to derive the certainty of a better life, and the hope of attaining it through daily exercise of our will. Such keenness of thought, such ecstasy of senses and spirit, must always have seemed to man as the best of all things good; that is why, in every age and every clime, he has considered only his immediate pleasure; and without regard to violating the laws of his constitution, he has looked to physical science, specifically to pharmaceutics, seeking in the coarsest liquors and the most subtle perfumes a means of escaping, if only for a few hours, from his earthen abode, and, as the author of Lazare expresses it, of "obtaining Paradise at a single shot". Alas! Man's vices, as filled with horror as they are thought to be, contain the proof (if only in their infinite spread!) of man's craving for infinity; only, it is a craving that often takes the wrong road. One could take the popular proverb, "All roads lead to Rome," in a metaphoric sense, and apply it to the realm of morality; everything leads to reward or punishment, the two forms of eternity. The human mind is running over with passions; it has "enough and to spare," if I may avail myself of another trivial locution; but this same unhappy mind (whose natural depravity is as great as its sudden, almost paradoxical capacity for generosity and the most demanding virtues) is teeming with paradoxes that permit it to turn the overflow of its excess passion to evil use. Man never believes that he is selling himself outright. In his infatuation, he forgets that he is gambling himself to a subtler and stronger one than he, and that, even when one yields but a single hair, the Spirit of Evil is not long in carrying off the entire head. And so, the visible lord of visible nature (I am speaking of man) has sought to create Paradise through pharmacy, and through fermented beverages, like some maniac who would replace solid furniture and real gardens with scenery painted on canvas and mounted on a frame. In my opinion, it is in this corruption of the meaning of infinity that lies the reason for all sinful intemperance, from the solitary, self-absorbed intoxication of a certain literary man (who had been obliged to seek relief from physical pain in opium, and so finding it a source of morbid pleasure, had gradually made it his only habit – the light of his spiritual life,) to the lowest, most repugnant drunk that rolls in the filth of the gutter, his brain afire.

Of the preparations best suited to create what I call the artificial Ideal (not counting liquor, which quickly provokes a man to a very unspiritual frenzy, and crushes his spiritual force; or perfume, which, if used excessively, will gradually exhaust a man's physical forces, even as it refines his imagination), the two strongest substances, as well as the ones that are most convenient to use and most readily obtainable, are hashish and opium. For the present, I will speak only of hashish; and this I will do in accordance with precise and extensive information, drawn from the notes and confidences of intelligent men who had long been devoted to it. Only I will incorporate these various documents into a sort of monograph, fixing on one single, easily characterized individual, as a type well-suited to experiences of this sort.

II.

What Is Hashish?

The accounts of Marco Polo, once unjustly ridiculed, have, like those of other travelers of antiquity, been verified by scholars, and merit our credence. I will not retell his story of how the Old Man of the Mountain confined a select number of his youngest disciples – those to whom he wished to give a hint of Paradisein a garden filled with delights, having first intoxicated them with hashish (whence, Hashishins or Assassins) – a sort of foretaste of reward for passive and unquestioning obedience. The reader may find information concerning the secret society of Hashishins by consulting von Hammer's book, and Sylvestre de Sacy's treatise, contained in Volume XVI of *Memoires de l'Académie des Inscriptions et Belles-Lettres;* concerning the etymology of the word "assassin", the reader is directed to de Sacy's letter to the editor of the *Moniteur,* appearing in issue number 359 of 1809. Herodotus tells us that the Scythians used to pile up hemp seeds, over which they would toss red-hot stones. For them, this was like a vapour bath, but far more fragrant than that of any Grecian steam room; they so delighted in it that they could not restrain their cries of joy.

Hashish does indeed come to us from the Orient; the stimulating properties of hemp were well-known in ancient Egypt, and its use is quite widespread, under different names, in India, Algeria, and Arabia. Even so, quite near at hand, under our very eyes, we have curious examples of intoxication caused by plant emanations. Without even considering the children who frequently experience strange dizzy spells after playing and rolling about in piles of alfalfa-mowings, we know that when the hemp is harvested, male and female workers alike sustain similar effects; it would seem as if a miasma were arising maliciously from the harvest to trouble their minds. The reaper's head spins in a vortex, and he is sometimes disturbed by dreams. At times, his limbs grow weak, and will not serve him. We have heard of rather frequent fits of sleepwalking among Russian peasants, and we are told that the cause must be attributed to their use of hempseed oil in food preparation. And who is unaware of the wild behavior of chickens who have eaten hemp seeds, or the fiery transports of horses who have been prepared for the steeple-chase, at weddings or on patron saints' days, by peasants who have given them a ration of hemp seeds, possibly sprinkled with wine?

French hemp, however, is unfit for conversion to hashish, or at least, according to repeated experiments, unfit to yield a drug equal in power to hashish. Hashish, or Indian hemp (*cannabis indica*), is a plant of the family *Urticaceae*, similar in every respect to our local variety, except that it does not reach the same height. It possesses the most extraordinary intoxicating properties, which have for several years attracted the attention of both scientists and the fashionable set in France. It is valued more or less highly, depending on its place of origin; that of Bengal is held in highest esteem by connoisseurs; but hashish from Egypt, Constantinople, Persia, and Algeria also possesses the same properties, though to a lesser degree.

Hashish (or grass, that is to say grass *par excellence,* as if the Arabs had wanted to describe *the* grass, source of every incorporeal sensual delight, in a single word) is known by various names, depending on its composition and the method of preparation to which it was subjected in the country in which it was harvested: in India it is known as *bangie*; in Africa, as *teriaki*; in Algeria and Arabia, as *madjound*, etc. The time of year at which it is harvested is not without consequence; it is when it is in flower that it possesses its greatest energy; the flowering tops are consequently the only parts used in the various preparations that we will have occasion to speak of.

Hashish *concentrate*, such as the Arabs prepare it, is obtained by boiling the tops of the flowering plant in butter with a little water. Following complete evaporation of all moisture, it is strained, and yields a preparation that looks like a greenish-yellow pomade, and retains the disagreeable odor of hashish and rancid butter. In this form it is taken in small balls of two to four grams; but because of the repugnant odor, which increases with time, the Arabs set the concentrate in the form of jellies.

The commonest of these jellies, *dawamesk*, is a mixture of concentrate, sugar, and various aromatics, such as vanilla, cinnamon, pistachio, almond, or musk. Occasionally, one even adds a bit of Spanish Fly, with an end in mind that has nothing whatever in common with the ordinary results of hashish. In this new form, there is nothing disagreeable in hashish, and one may take it – either done up in a wafer or dissolved in a cup of coffee – in doses of 15, 20, even 30 grams.

The experiments conducted by Smith, Gastinel, and Décourtive were intended to arrive at the discovery of the active element of hashish. Despite their efforts, its chemical combination is still little known; but its properties are generally attributed to a resinous matter that it contains in rather large quantities, in the proportion of about ten parts per 100. To obtain this resin, the dried plant is ground into a coarse powder, and washed several times with alcohol, which is then partially removed by distillation; the liquid is evaporated until the consistency of an extract is attained; this extract is treated with water, which dissolves any gummy foreign matter, leaving the resin in its pure state.

This product is soft, dark green in color, and possesses the characteristic odor of hashish to a high degree. Five, ten, or fifteen centigrams are enough to produce surprising effects. But like dawamesk and hashish concentrate, *cannabin*, which may be taken in the form of chocolate pellets or little ginger pills, produces effects of greater or lesser strength, and of a highly variant nature, conforming to individual temperament and nervous sensitivity. Or, more correctly, the result varies even within the same individual. Sometimes it will be an excessive, irresistible merriment, sometimes a sensation of well-being and fullness of life, sometimes a restless, dream-fraught sleep. All the same, there are phenomena which recur fairly regularly, especially among people who share a common temperament and educational background; there is a kind of unity in the diversity, and it is this which will permit me without too much difficulty to draft the monograph on intoxication to which I referred above.

In Constantinople, in Algeria, even in France, there are those who smoke hashish mixed with tobacco; but in this case the phenomena in question occur only in a slack and "sluggish" form. I have heard that a certain essential oil, which seems to contain an active force greater than that of any preparation known to date, has recently been extracted from hashish by distillation; but it has not been studied enough for me to be able to speak with certainty of its effects. It would be superfluous to add that tea, coffee, and spirits are powerful adjuvants which, to a greater or lesser degree, accelerate the advent of this mysterious intoxication.

III.

The Seraphic Theatre

What do you feel? What do you see? Are there wonderful things, extraordinary visions? Is it very beautiful? and very terrible? and very dangerous? – Such are the usual questions that the uninitiated put to the experienced user, prompted by a curiosity mixed with fear. They seem to have a childlike impatience for knowledge, like that of people who have never left their own hearthside, when they find themselves in the presence of a man who has just returned from distant, unknown lands. They imagine hashish intoxication as a wondrous land, a vast theater of magic and juggling where everything is miraculous and unexpected. That is a preconceived notion, a total misconception. And since, for the average reader and enquirer, the word *hashish* carries with it the idea of a strange and topsy-turvy world, and the expectation of wondrous dreams (it would be better to say "hallucinations," which are, moreover, less frequent than one would suppose), I will here and now indicate the important difference which separates the effects of hashish from the marvels of sleep. In sleep, that nightly voyage of adventure, there is something positively miraculous; it is a miracle whose regularity has dulled the edges of its mystery. Man's dreams are of two kinds. The first, filled with details of his ordinary life – his preoccupations, his desires, his vices – combine, in a more or less bizarre manner with things glimpsed during the day, which have been imprinted at random on the vast backdrop of his memory. That is natural dream; it is the man himself. Ah, but the other kind of dream! The absurd, unexpected dream, that lacks bearing or connection with the character, the life and the passions of the dreamer! this dream, which I will call "hieroglyphic", evidently represents the supernatural side of life, and it is precisely because it was absurd that the ancients believed in its divinity. As it was inexplicable in terms of natural causes, they attributed an extra-human cause to it; and even today, dream interpreters aside, there is still a philosophic school which sees in dreams of this type sometimes reproach, sometimes counsel; in short, a moral and symbolic tableau generated in the very soul of the sleeping man. It is a dictionary that must be studied, a language whose key may be had by the wise.

In hashish intoxication, there is nothing like this. We will not leave the province of natural dream. It is true that, throughout its duration, the intoxication will be nothing but one immense

187

dream, thanks to intensity of color and the rapidity of conceptions; but it will always preserve the particular tonality of the individual. A man has sought to dream, and dream will overcome him; but the dream will certainly reflect its dreamer. The idle fellow has contrived to introduce the unusual into his life and thoughts by artificial means; but after all, and in spite of the accidental vitality of his sensations, he is only the same man grown larger, the same number raised to a very high power.

He has been dominated, but by his ill luck, it was only by himself-that is to say, by the part of himself that was already dominant. He wanted to play the angel, he has in point of fact become a beast, monentarily very powerful, if, at any rate, one may refer to an extreme sensitivity, without the control to moderate or exploit it, as "power".

Let it be known, then, by both sophisticate and *ingénu* out to find exceptional pleasure, that in hashish they will find nothing miraculous, absolutely nothing but the natural to an extreme. The mind and body upon which hashish operates will yield only their ordinary, personal phenomena, increased, it is true, in amount and vitality, but still faithful to their original. Man will not escape the fate of his physical and mental nature: to his impressions and intimate thoughts, hashish will be a magnifying mirror, but a *true* mirror, nonetheless.

Here is the drug beneath your eyes: a bit of green jelly, equal in bulk to a walnut, strange-smelling, to the point that it arouses a certain repulsion and a faint hint of nausea, as, moreover, would any subtle – even agreeable – odor, brought to its maximum force and density, as it were. Let me remark, in passing, that this proposition may be reversed, such that the most repugnant, the most revolting odor might become a pleasure, were it reduced to the slightest possible amount and expansiveness. – This, then, is happiness! It occupies the volume of a little spoon! Happiness with all its intoxication, all its folly, all its childishness! You may swallow without fear; it won't kill you. Your bodily organs will be done no harm by it. Later on, perhaps, your strength of will may be diminished by too frequent recourse to this charm, and perhaps you will be less of a man than you are today: but punishment is so far off, and the future disaster is by nature so hard to define! What risk are you taking? a little nervous fatigue tomorrow. Do you not risk greater punishment every day for lesser rewards? There, it is said: you have even diluted your dose of concentrate in a cup of black coffee, so as to give it greater strength and expansiveness; you have been careful to free your stomach, postponing your heavy meal until nine or ten at night, so that you may allow the poison complete freedom of action; at most, in an hour you will have some light soup. You now have sufficient ballast for a long, strange journey. The whistle has blown, the sails are set, and you have over ordinary travellers the curious advantage of not knowing where you are going. You asked for it; here's to fate!

I presume that you have taken the precaution to choose the moment for this little adventure trip carefully. Any perfect debauche requires perfect leisure. Moreover, you know that hashish exaggerates not only the individual, but circumstances and settings as well. You have no tasks demanding punctuality or precision to execute; no family problem; no lovesickness. One must be careful. That problem, that uneasiness, that nagging memory of a task requiring your determination and attention at a given moment, would come knelling through your reverie to taint your pleasure. Uneasiness would turn to anguish; a slight problem would become a torture. If, once all the preliminary conditions have been met, the weather turns out to be fine; and if you should happen to find yourself in favorable surroundings, such as a picturesque countryside, or a poetically decorated apartment; and if, in addition, you can expect a little music, then everything is going just fine.

Generally speaking, hashish intoxication passes through three readily distinguishable phases, and to the new user, the first symptoms of the first phase prove of something more than passing interest. You have heard, in very sketchy terms, of the wonderful effects of hashish; your imagination has preconceived a specific idea of something like the perfect intoxication; you're all eagerness to know whether the reality will come up to your expectations. That alone is enough to throw you, right at the start, into a state of anxiety, which is quite favorable to the invading and conquering disposition of the poison. During the first stage of their intoxication, most new users complain of the long delay in manifestation of the effects; they await the first signs with a childlike impatience, and when they find that the drug is not working quickly enough to suit them, they give way to great swaggering professions of incredulity, which always amuse the experienced users who know how hashish operates. The earliest symptoms, like the signs of a storm that has been hovering for a long while, appear in the very lap of this incredulity. At first, there is a certain absurd, irresistible hilarity that overcomes you. These unprovoked paroxysms of mirth, of which you are almost ashamed, recur frequently, interrupting periods of stupor during which you try in vain to collect yourself. The most ordinary words, the most trivial ideas, assume a new and bizarre aspect; you are even surprised at having found them so commonplace until now. Incongruous, unpredictable equations and comparisons, endless puns, and comic sketches keep gushing from your brain. The demon has invaded you; it is useless to resist this hilarity, which racks you like a good tickling. Now and again you break out laughing at yourself, and at your own silliness and foolery; and your comrades, if you should have any, also laugh at your condition, and their own; but as they are without malice, you do not resent them for it.

The mirth (which alternately tapers off and gallops forward at top speed), the uneasiness you feel even in your joy, the insecurity, the on-again, off-again quality of the ailment – all generally last only a fairly short time. Soon, the relations between ideas become so vague, the conductor-wire that connects your thoughts grows so tenuous, that only your fellows can understand you. And again, on this score, there is no means of verification: Perhaps they only *believe* they understand you, and the impression is mutual. The frolics and the bursts of laughter, not unlike explosions, seem to be true madness, or at least maniacal foolishness, to anyone who is not in the same condition as you. By the same token, the discretion, good sense and regular thinking of the cautious onlooker who has not become intoxicated, delights and amuses you as a very special kind of lunacy. The roles have been reversed. His composure spurs you on to the final extremes of sarcasm. It is indeed an unexplainably funny situation – is it not? – when a man is enjoying a merriment that is incomprehensible to any outsider. The madman takes pity on the sane, and it is then that the idea of his superiority begins to dawn on the horizon of his mind. By and by it will swell, expand, and flare up like a meteor.

I was once witness to a scene of this sort that was carried very far – a scene in which the grotesque was intelligible only to people who understood, at least through having observed it in others, the effects of the substance, and the enormous difference in pitch that it creates between two supposedly equal intellects. A famous musician, who knew nothing of the properties of hashish, who perhaps had never even heard of it, happened into the midst of a gathering where several people had taken it. They tried to make him understand its marvellous effects. He smiled gracefully at their wondrous accounts – indulgently, like a man who is willing to pose for a few minutes. His contempt was quickly understood by all the minds that had been sharpened by the poison, and their laughter wounded him. The bursts of joy, the puns, the altered faces, the whole unhealthy atmosphere, irritated him, and provoked him to declare (perhaps sooner than he would have wanted) that the *burden* of this artistic joke was very bad, and that besides it must be quite exhausting for the people who were *carrying it out*. The humor of this flashed through all the minds like lightning. There was a redoubling of mirth. "This joke may be good for you," he said, "but for me, no." "It's quite enough that it should be good for *us*," one of the afflicted creatures selfishly replied. Not knowing whether he was dealing with genuine madmen or simply people who were feigning madness, our man felt that the wisest decision would be to leave; but someone locked the door and hid the key. Someone else, on his knees before him, asked his forgiveness on behalf of all the group, and insolently informed him (but with *tears* in his eyes) that, despite his intellectual inferiority, which might, perhaps, inspire a bit of pity, they were all moved by the deepest affection for him. The fellow resigned himself to staying, and, upon being pressed, even condescended to play some music. But the sounds of the violin, as they spread through the apartment like some new contagion, *gripped* (the word is not any too strong) now one affected creature, now another. There were deep, hoarse sighs, sudden sobs, streams of silent tears. The terrified musician stopped, and approaching the fellow whose ecstatic condition was creating the loudest uproar, he asked him whether he was suffering much, and what would be necessary to relieve him. One of the people about, a practical man, suggested lemonade and sours. But the hashish victim, the light of rapture in his eyes, looked at them both with unspeakable contempt. Fancy wanting to cure a man who is sick with joy, sick with too much life!

As may be seen by this anecdote, benevolence holds a rather large place in the feelings brought on by hashish; a slow, lazy, inarticulate benevolence that derives from a tendering of the nerves. In support of this observation, a certain person told me of an adventure that befell him while he was in this state of intoxication; and as he had kept a very precise memory of his feelings, I understood perfectly the ludicrous, unsolvable predicament into which he had been thrown by the difference of pitch and level of performance that I spoke of above. I do not recall whether the man in question was then trying hashish for the first or second time. Had he perhaps taken too strong a dose, or had the hashish, without any apparent help from other factors, produced, (as frequently happens,) effects far more intense than usual? He told me that even through his pleasure – that supreme pleasure of feeling full of life, and honestly believing that you are loaded with talent – he had suddenly hit upon a matter of some terror. At first dazzled by the beauty of his sensations, he had all at once grown frightened. He had wondered what would become of his mind and body if this condition, which he took for supernatural, were to go on getting worse and worse forever, and if his nerves were always to keep growing more and more delicate. Because of the magnifying power that the victim's mental eye possessed, this fear must have been an indescribable torture. "I was," said he, "like a runaway horse, heading top speed for the brink of a chasm, and wanting to stop, but not being able to do so. It was, indeed, a terrifying gallop; and my thoughts (slave to the circumstances and surroundings, to accident, and to everything that may be implied in the word 'chance') had taken a turn that was purely and simply rhapsodical. It is too late! I kept repeating over and over in despair. When I stopped feeling this way, after what seemed an infinity to me, but perhaps had only been a few minutes; when at last I felt able to yield completely to the quiet bliss (so dear to the Orientals) that succeeds this frenzied stage, I was overcome by yet another unhappy circumstance. A different anxiety, of a very trivial and childish nature, descended upon me. I suddenly remembered that I had been invited to dinner at an evening affair for a group of staid and solemn men. I envisioned myself in the midst of a reserved and sober crowd, where everyone was master of himself, and I alone was obliged (beneath the glare of many lamps) painstakingly to conceal my mental state. I certainly believed that I would manage it, but I also almost felt myself fainting when I thought of the strength of will that I would have to put into it. By some chance or other, the words of the Gospel, 'Woe to that man by whom the offence cometh!' had just surged into my memory; and though I wanted to forget them, though I really applied myself to forgetting them, I kept repeating them over and over in my mind. *My* woe (and woe it really was) assumed magnificent proportions. I resolved, despite my weakness, to muster up some energy and consult a pharmacist; for I didn't know the antidote, and I wanted to go to the gathering, where duty called me, with a free and unencumbered mind. But on the threshold of the druggist's shop, I was suddenly taken by a thought, which gave me pause for several seconds, and made me think. I had just caught sight of myself, in passing, in the glass of a shop-window, and my face had astounded me. The pallor, the lips driven inward, the widened eyes! I am going to worry this fine gentleman, said I to myself, and for such nonsense! Add to that the feeling of ridicule that I wanted to avoid, and the dread of finding anyone else in the shop. But my sudden spirit of goodwill for that unknown pharmacist dominated all my other feelings. I imagined that this man was as sensitive as I myself at this awful time; and as I also fancied that his ear and his soul must, like my own, vibrate at the slightest sound, I resolved to enter his shop on tip-toe. I told myself that I could not possibly show too much consideration in the presence of a man whose tenderheartedness I was just about to jolt. So then I promised myself that I would hush the sound of my voice, just as I would the noise of my footsteps; you know that hashish-voice, do you not? – heavy, deep and guttural, much like the voices of old opium-eaters. The result of all this was just the opposite of what I wanted to obtain. Determined to reassure the pharmacist, I ended by terrifying him. He knew nothing whatever about this 'ailment', had never even heard of it. But he kept looking at me with a curiosity that was heavily mixed with defiance. Did he take me for a madman, an evil-doer or a beggar? Doubtless neither one nor the other; but all these absurd ideas crossed my mind. I was obliged to explain to him, at great length (and how tedious that was!), exactly what hemp jelly was, and what it was used for; I repeated to him, over and over, that there was no danger, no reason for *him* to be alarmed, and that all I was asking was some way of softening or counteracting its effects; I kept stressing my sincere regret at causing him such bother. In the end – and try to understand all the humiliation that these words held for me – he simply asked me *to leave*. Such was the reward for my excessive kindheartedness and goodwill. I went to my evening affair; I offended no-one. No-one guessed the superhuman efforts that I needed to exert to seem like everybody else. But I will never forget the torture of an ultra-poetic intoxication, impeded by decorum and thwarted by a sense of obligation!"

Although I naturally tend to sympathize with any suffering that is born of the imagination, I cannot help but laugh at this account. The man who gave it to me has not been reformed. He has continued to seek from that accursed jelly the stimulation that he should find from within himself; but, as he is a steady, cautious man, a man of the world, he has lessened the doses, which has permitted him to increase their frequency. Later on, he will enjoy the rotten fruits of his habit.

I return to the regular evolution of the intoxication. After this first stage of childish merriment, there is something like a temporary lull. But new events are soon ushered in by a coldish sensation in the extremities (which, in certain individuals, may even become very intensely cold), and by a great weakness throughout the body; you are butter-fingered, and you feel an embarrassing numbness and a stupefaction in your head, and throughout your being. Your eyes dilate; they seem drawn in every direction by an implacable ecstasy. Your face is drained of color. Your lips contract and turn inward on your mouth, with the panting motion that characterizes the aspirations of a man caught up in great schemes, weighed down by vast thoughts, or catching his breath before taking off for a leap. Your throat seems to be closing. Your palate is dried by a thirst that it would be infinitely sweet to quench, were it not that the pleasure of indolence was even sweeter, and basically opposed to the slightest disturbance of your body. Deep, hoarse sighs burst from your chest, as if your old body were unable to bear the intense activity and strange desires of your new soul. From time to time, a shudder runs through you, causing an involuntary motion, like the sudden starts that come before deep sleep, at the end of a working day or on a stormy night.

Before going any further, I would like to tell yet another anecdote, that relates to the coldish sensation that I spoke of above, and will serve to show the extent to which the effects – even the purely *physical* ones – can vary according to the individual. This time, it is a man of letters who is speaking, and in certain passages of the narrative, I believe the reader will be able to find indications of a literary temperament.

"I had taken a moderate dose of concentrate," this gentleman told me, "and everything was going just fine. The fit of unwholesome hilarity had lasted only a short while, and I was in a state of listless amazement, which amounted almost to happiness. So I promised myself a tranquil, carefree evening. Unfortunately, as luck would have it, I was obliged to accompany someone to the theatre. I made my decision bravely, and resolved to hide my enormous desire for laziness and inertia. As all of the carriages in my neighborhood had been reserved, I had to resign myself to a long journey on foot, through the dissonant noises of traffic, the stupid conversation of passers-by, and a whole ocean of trivialities. A slight coolness had already appeared in the tips of my fingers; this soon turned to a very stinging cold, as if I had both my hands dipped in a bucket of ice water. But it was no cause to suffer; rather, the almost piercing sensation pervaded me with pleasure. Yet it seemed that this coldness was spreading over me more and more, as I proceeded on my endless journey. Two or three times I asked the person in whose company I was whether it was really very cold; he replied that, quite to the contrary, the weather was something more than warm. When I was finally settled in the theatre, hidden away in the box reserved for me, with three or four hours of rest before me, I felt as if I had arrived at the Promised Land. The feelings that I had held back along the way, with all the meagre energy that I could possibly muster, now overflowed, and I indulged, without restraint, in my wordless frenzy. The cold was still increasing, and yet I saw people lightly dressed, and even wiping their foreheads with a tired air. I was taken by the amusing idea that I was a privileged person, a man who, alone, had been granted the right to feel cold in a playhouse on a summer night. The cold kept growing, to the point where it became alarming; but I was, above all, governed by my curiosity to know just how low it could go. Finally, it came so far, and was so complete, so general, that all my thoughts froze, as it were; I was a chunk of thinking ice; I looked upon myself as a statue hewn of a single block of ice; and this mad hallucination gave me a certain pride, and inspired in me a certain mental comfort that I would not know how to describe to you. What added to the abominable pleasure that I had from this, was the certainty that no one present knew my nature, or even the superiority that I held over them; and then there was the joy of thinking that my companion had not, for a single second, suspected the bizarre sensations that possessed me! I had the reward for my dissimulation, and my exceptional pleasure remained a true secret.

"For the rest, I had hardly entered my box when my eyes were struck by an impression of darkness, which seemed to have some kinship with the idea of cold. It may well be that the two ideas lent each other force. You know that hashish always craves magnificent shows of light – glorious splendors, cascades of liquid gold; all light is good – light that streams down in sheets, and light that catches like tinsel in the little nooks and crannies; the candelabra of Society, the little tapers lit for Mary, and the avalanche of rose in sunsets. It seemed that the one miserable chandelier shed a light that was wholly insufficient for my insatiable thirst for brightness; I thought, as I have said, that I was entering a world of darkness, which, moreover, closed in thick about me, as I dreamt of polar night and endless winter. The stage (designed for a comedy) alone was brightly lit, and seemed infinitely small and far, far away, as if at the end of an immense stereoscope. I will not try to tell you that I *listened* to the players; you know that's quite impossible; now and then, my stream of thought would seize upon some sentence fragment, and, like an able dancer, would use it as a trampoline, to spring to distant dreams. You might suppose that a play heard in this way would lack logic and connection; allow me to enlighten you; I found a very subtle meaning in the drama spun by my distracted state of mind. Nothing fazed me; I was something like the poet who, on seeing *Esther* played for the first time, found it quite natural that

195

Haman should declare his love to the queen. As may be guessed, it was at the moment that he threw himself at Esther's feet to beg pardon for his crimes. If all plays were heard in this way, they would gain great beauty by it even the plays of Racine.

"The players seemed extremely small to me, and carefully, precisely outlined, like the figures of Meissonier. I distinctly perceived, not only the minutest details of their attire, such as fabric patterns, seams and buttons, but also the line of separation between the false face and the real – the rouge and powder and every sort of make-up. And these Lilliputians were cloaked in a cold and magic light, much like the kind that a very clear pane of glass will add to an oil painting. When at last I was able to emerge from this pit of frozen darkness; when the internal phantasmagoria had disappeared, and I was Myself once again, I felt a lassitude far greater than any that sustained hard work had ever caused me."

It is, in fact, at this stage of the intoxication that a new sharpness – a greater keenness – becomes apparent in all the senses. The senses of smell, sight, hearing and touch alike participate in this development. One's eyes focus on infinity. One's ear perceives near-imperceptible sounds in the very midst of the loudest tumult. It is then that the hallucinations begin. One by one, external objects slowly assume strange appearances; they grow shapeless and reshape themselves. Next occur the ambiguities, the shuffling and misunderstanding of ideas. Sounds are clad in color, and colors contain a certain music. This, you will say, is only quite natural, and any poetic mind, in its normal rational state, will easily comprehend such analogies. But I have already informed the reader that there is nothing exactly supernatural in hashish intoxication; it is only that now the analogies assume an unaccustomed vividness; they attack, pervade, and overcome the mind with their despotic character. Musical notes become numbers, and if your mind is endowed with any mathematical ability, the melody, the music that you hear, will be transformed (while still preserving its sensual, voluptuous nature) into one vast- arithmetical operation, in which numbers engender other numbers, as you follow the cycles of their generation with inexplicable ease, and an agility equal to that of the performer.

It sometimes happens that your individual identity will disappear, and the objectivity characteristic of the pantheistic poets will develop so unusually within you, that the mere contemplation of external objects will cause you soon to forget your own existence, and become inextricably fused with theirs. Your eye fastens upon a tree that sings as it is bent by the wind; in a few seconds, something that would be a most natural comparison in the poet's mind, will become a *reality* in yours. First, you will attribute your passions, longings, and sadnesses to the tree; its moaning and swaying will become your own; and by and by, *you are the tree, itself*. Similarly, the bird that is soaring high in the blue, begins by representing the age-old desire to soar above the things of man; but now, already, you have become the bird, itself. I am imagining you sitting and smoking. Your attention will settle for a bit too long upon the bluish clouds that are being exhaled from your pipe. The notion of a slow, on-going, eternal burning-off will take possession of your mind, and soon you will adapt this notion to your own thoughts, your "thinking-matter". By a strange shuffling process, a sort of intellectual transposition or *quid pro quo, you* will feel *yourself* going up in smoke, and you will invest your pipe (in which you believe you are huddled and crouching like so much tobacco,) with the extraordinary ability of *smoking you.*

Luckily, this interminable imagining turns out to have lasted only for a minute; for a lucid interval, and a great expenditure of effort, have permitted you to take a look at the clock. But another stream of ideas sweeps you away; it will roll you along for yet another minute in its rushing whirlwind; and this other minute will become one more eternity. For temporal and existential proportions are disturbed by the multiplicity and intensity of your feelings and ideas. It would seem as if you were living several lifetimes in the space of an hour. Are you not, then, much like some fantastic novel that insists on coming to life, instead of staying *written?* There is no longer any relationship between your body and the pleasure; and it is particularly from this consideration that arises any blame applicable to this dangerous practice, wherein one's liberty is lost.

When I speak of hallucinations, the word ought not to be taken in its strictest sense. A most important nuance distinguishes the *true* hallucination, such as physicians have often found occasion to study it, from the hallucination – or rather, the sensory misinterpretation-of the mental state brought on by hashish. In the first instance, the hallucination is sudden, inevitable, and complete; furthermore, it finds no pretext or excuse for happening in the world of external objects. The person afflicted by it will see a form or hear a sound where, in reality, there is none. In the second instance, the hallucination is progressive, almost voluntary, and becomes complete and perfect only through the operation of imagination. Lastly, it has a pretext for existing. Sounds will speak, and say things quite distinctly; but sounds indeed there were. The drunken eye of a man drunk on hashish will see strange forms; but

197

before these forms grew strange and monstrous, they were simply natural. The strength, the truly expressive vividness of the hallucination that occurs in intoxication, in no way weakens this fundamental difference. The one has roots in the immediate surroundings, and the present time; the other has none.

So that I may help the reader to better understand this bubblingover of imagination, as well as the progressive maturation of the dream and the poetic bringing-forth to which a brain grown drunk on hashish is condemned, I will tell yet another anecdote. This time, it is not an idle young man who is speaking, nor is it a man of letters; it is a woman – a woman a bit on in years, inquisitive, and somewhat excitable by nature; she had given in to her desire to become acquainted with the poisonous stuff, and she describes her main vision to another lady, in the following manner. (I am transcribing word for word.)

"However strange and fresh and new might have been the sensations that I derived from the twelve-hour (twelve or twenty? I really don't know!) folly of my intoxication, I will not repeat them any more. The mental stimulation is too acute, and the resultant fatigue is far too great; and, in a word, I find something criminal in this childishness. In short, I gave in to my curiosity; and then, there was a kind of general lunacy going on, at the home of some old friends, and I saw no great harm in a little lack of dignity. First of all, I must tell you that this accursed hashish is a most perfidious substance; you sometimes think that you are quit of the intoxication, but it is only a deceitful calm. There are periods of peace, and then renewal of the disorders. Thus, toward ten o'clock at night, I found myself in one of those temporary quiet states; I thought that I had been delivered from the superabundance of life that had given me so much pleasure, it is true, but that still had not been without some anxiety and fear. I sat down to supper with much pleasure, like one wearied by a long voyage. For until then, I had cautiously abstained from eating. But before I had even risen from table, my delirium had once more seized me, as a cat would a mouse, and the poison again began to play with my poor brain. Although my house is located only a short distance from our friends' chateau, and although there was a carriage at my disposal, I felt so completely overcome by the need to dream and to give way to this irresistible folly, that I joyfully accepted the offer that they made to keep me over until the next day. You're familiar with the chateau; you know that they've renovated, decorated and spruced up the whole part inhabited by the owners with the very latest fixings; but the part that is usually uninhabited has been left as is, with its old styling and old decorations. It was decided that they would improvise a bedroom for me in this part of the chateau, and to that end, they chose the smallest room, a sort of boudoir, which was a bit faded and worn, but no less charming for all that. I must describe it to you as well as I am able, so that you can understand the strange vision that I was prey to-a vision that obsessed me for an entire night, and left me no leisure to perceive the flight of time.

"This boudoir is very small, very narrow. Just above the cornice, the ceiling rounds and becomes vaulted; the walls are covered with long, narrow mirrors, eparated by panels painted with landscapes done in the loose style of theatrical scenery. On a level with the cornice, on all four walls, are depicted various allegorical figures, some reclining, others running or flying about. Above them, some brilliantly-colored birds and flowers. Behind the figures, a deceptively painted trellis-work rises, following the natural curve of the ceiling. The ceiling is gilded. Thus, all the space between the cornice-rod and the figures is covered with gold, and at the center of the ceiling the gold is interrupted only by the geometric interlacings of the mock-trellis. You can see that all this is a little like a very distinguished cage, a very beautiful cage for a very big bird. I must add that the night was very lovely, very clear, and the moon very bright, so much so that, even after I had put out the candle, all of this decoration remained visible, lit - not by my mind's eye, as you might believe - but by the splendor of the night, whose gleamings caught upon all the golden, mirrored, gaudy-colored adornment of the place.

"I was at first astonished to see great, wide spaces stretch out before me, about me, on all sides; there were clear rivers and verdant countrysides mirrored in the still waters. You understand that this was the effect of the panels reflected by the mirrors. When I lifted my eyes, I saw a setting sun that resembled molten metal growing cold again. It was the gold of the ceiling; but the lattice-work led me to believe that I was in a kind of cage or house that opened on all sides to Space, and that nothing separated me from all these wonders but the bars of my magnificent prison. At first, I laughed at this illusion; but the longer I looked, the more the magic increased, and the greater the life and transparency and despotic reality it all assumed. From this point on, the idea of confinement dominated my thoughts, but, I must admit, without much standing in the way of the various pleasures I derived from the spectacle stretched out around and above me. I thought of myself as having long been locked away - for thousands of years, perhaps - in this sumptuous cage, amidst enchanting landscapes, and surrounded by a wondrous horizon. I dreamed of *Sleeping Beauty*, and of an atonement that must be undergone, and of future deliverance. Brilliant tropical birds flew above my head; and, as my hearing perceived the distant sound of little bells about the necks of horses who were proceeding, far away, along the highway, the two senses blended their impressions into a single idea, and I attributed the mysterious, tinkling song to the birds, imagining that they sang with metal throats. Evidently, they were speaking about me, rejoicing in my captivity. Groups of frolicking monkeys and clowning satyrs seemed to be amusing themselves at the expense of the poor prisoner, who lay stretched out flat, condemned to immobility. But all the mythological divinities looked upon me with a charming smile, as if to encourage me to bear this sorcery with patience; and they all rolled their eyes sideways, as if to catch my look. I concluded from this that if some ancient failing, some sin unknown even to me, had necessitated such a temporary punishment, I could still count on some superior Goodness who, while dooming me to endless caution, would still offer me more serious diversion than the dollhouse fun that filled our childhood days. You can see that moral considerations were not absent from my dream; but I must confess that the pleasure of contemplating those shapes and brilliant colors, and of believing myself to be the center of some fantastic drama, frequently absorbed all my other thoughts. This state lasted for a long, long while... Did it last until morning? I don't know. I suddenly saw the morning sun full in my room; I felt a keen sense of astonishment, and despite all the effort that I could put forth to remember, it was impossible for me to tell if I had slept or had patiently passed through a delicious insomnia. A moment ago, it was night, and now – daylight! And yet, I had lived... oh! through such a long, long time!... Since the notion of time, or rather, the *dimension* of time, had been abolished, the entire night was measurable for me only by the multiplicity of my thoughts. However long it should have appeared from this point of view, it sometimes seemed to me that it had lasted only a few seconds, or even that it had never taken place at all.

"I won't even mention my exhaustion to you... it was immense. They say that the rapture of poets and creative sorts is much like what I felt, although I have always fancied that people charged with the task of exciting our emotions must be endowed with a very calm temperament; but if poetic delirium resembles what a little teaspoonful of jelly got for me, then I think that it must cost the poets very dear to delight their public; and it was not without a certain sense of comfort, a kind of prosaic satisfaction, that I at last felt myself *at home,* in my mental *at home,* by which I mean back in the real world."

There we have a woman who obviously makes sense; but we will use her account only to extract a few useful notes, which will serve to round out this highly abridged description of the principal sensations produced by hashish.

She spoke of supper as a pleasure that came just at the right time, at the moment that a temporary (but seemingly definitive) lull allowed her to step back into the real world. Indeed, there are, as I have said, intermissions and deceptive calms; and hashish often causes a voracious appetite, and almost always an excessive thirst. Only, instead of bringing an enduring peace, dinner or supper will create just such a new seizure, just such a dizzying attack as the one this lady complained of; in this instance, it was followed by a series of beguiling visions, lightly tinged with fear, to which she resigned herself quite positively, and with very good grace. The tyrannical hunger and thirst of which we are speaking here cannot be satisfied without a certain amount of labor. For a man feels so far above material considerations, or rather, he is so completely overcome by his intoxication, that he must display a great deal of very trying courage, just to lift a bottle or a fork.

The final attack brought on by digestion of food is indeed most violent: it is impossible to struggle against it; and a state of this sort would be unbearable if it were to last too long, and did not soon yield to another stage of the intoxication, which, in the case cited above, was expressed in terms of splendid, mildly terrifying visions, which still held many consolations. This new state is what the Orientals call *kief.* There is no longer anything rushing and tumultuous; there's a calm placid beatitude, a glorious resignation. Long since you have ceased to be your own master, but you are no longer troubled by this. Your suffering and your idea of time have disappeared; or if they should dare to present themselves, it is only in a form transfigured by your dominant feeling; so that, in relation to their customary form, they are what a bit of poetic melancholy is to positive grief.

But, above all, let us note that in this lady's account (and it is because of this that I transcribed it) the hallucination is of a bastardized nature, and derives its reason for existence from the scenery without; the mind is but a mirror where the immediate surroundings are reflected back, exceedingly transformed. Next, we are going to interpose the question of what I would like to call the moral hallucination: our subject felt that she was undergoing an atonement; but the female temperament, which is hardly suited to analysis, did not permit her to take note of the singularly optimistic nature of her hallucination. The kindly look of the Olympean deities has been idealized by an essentially hashishistic glaze. I will not say that this lady narrowly escaped remorse; but her thoughts, which for a moment turned to melancholy and regret, were very rapidly colored by hope. This is an observation which we will have still other occasion to verify.

She spoke of the exhaustion of the following day; indeed, this exhaustion is great, but it does not appear immediately, and when you are obliged to recognize it, it is not without some astonishment. For at first, when you have ascertained that a new day has risen over the horizon of your life, you feel an amazing wellbeing; you think that you are possessed of a wonderful lightness of spirit. But hardly are you on your feet, when a trace of the old intoxication follows you and holds you back, like the ball-and-chain of your recent servitude. Your feeble legs guide you timidly, and from moment to moment you are afraid of breaking yourself like some fragile object. A great languor (and there are those who claim that it is not lacking in charm) grips your spirit, and spreads through your mind like mist across the countryside. There you are, for several hours more, incapable of work or energy or any positive action. Such is the punishment for the ungodly wastefulness with which you have squandered all your nervous energy. You have strewn your personality in all directions, and now, what difficulty you are having in putting it back together again!

IV.

The Man-God

It is time to set aside all this jugglery, all these great marionettes, born of the dreams of childish minds. There are more serious things for us to speak of, are there not? –the changes that occur in human feelings, and, in a word, the "morality" of hashish.

Thus far, I have done only a short study of the intoxication; I have limited myself to highlighting its main features, particularly the concrete ones. But more important for an intellectual, I believe, is to know how the posion acts upon man's mental faculties – that is to say, how it causes a magnification, distortion, and exaggeration of his usual feelings and moral perceptions, which come to exhibit really amazing refraction, under the exceptional atmospheric conditions.

A man who, having long indulged in opium or hashish, has been able to find the strength necessary to free himself, even weakened as he was by his enslaving habit, appears to me much like an escaped prisoner. He inspires far more admiration in me than the prudent man who has never gone astray, always taking care to avoid temptation. The English often apply certain terms to opium-eaters which can seem excessive only to the naïve souls who do not know the horrors of this particular form of decadence: "enchained, fettered, enslaved!" Chains, indeed, beside which all the others – chains of Duty, chains of Illicit Love – are but threads of gossamer and spider's webs! Dread union of man with himself! "I had become a bounden slave in the trammels of opium, and my labors and my orders had taken a coloring from my dreams," says Ligeia's husband; but was not Poe (that incomparable poet, that irrefutable philosopher, who must always be quoted on questions of mysterious mental ailments) actually describing the dark, intriguing splendors of opium in any number of wonderful passages? Egaeus the metaphysician, lover of the radiant Berenice, speaks of an alteration in his mental faculties, which constrained him to invest the simplest phenomena with an unnatural and monstrous importance:

"To muse for long unwearied hours, with my attention riveted to some frivolous device on the margin or in the typography of a book; to become absorbed for the better part of a summer's day, in a quaint shadow falling aslant upon the tapestry or upon the floor; to lose myself, for an entire night, in watching the steady flame of a lamp, or the embers of a fire; to dream away whole days over the perfume of a flower; to repeat, monotonously, some common word, until the sound, by dint of frequent repetition, ceased to convey any idea whatever to the mind; ... such were a few of the most common and least pernicious vagaries induced by a condition of the mental faculties, not, indeed, altogether unparalleled, but certainly bidding defiance to any thing like analysis or explanation."

And the nervous Augustus Bedloe, who swallows his dose of opium every day before his morning walk, admits that the chief benefit he derives from this daily poisoning is that of taking an exaggerated interest in all things-even the most trivial:

"In the meantime the morphine had its customary effect – that of enduing all the external world with an intensity of interest. In the quivering of a leaf – in the hue of a blade of grass – in the shape of a trefoil – in the humming of a bee – in the gleaming of a dewdrop – in the breathing of the wind – in the faint odors that came from the forest – there came a whole universe of suggestion – a bright and varied train of rhapsodical and immethodical thought."

Thus did the prince of mystery, the master of horror, express himself through the mouths of his characters. Both those characteristics of opium are perfectly applicable to hashish; with the one, as with the other, man's intellect, once free, becomes enslaved; but that word "rhapsodical", which so well describes a train of thoughts inspired and controlled by the outer world and chance circumstances, is truer and more terrible in the case of hashish. There, one's ability to reason is no more than a wreck, at the mercy of all tides, and the train of thoughts is infinitely more accelerated and more rhapsodical. Which is to say, clearly enough, I believe, that hashish, in this particular effect, is far more powerful than opium, far more injurious to regular living – in a word, far more disturbing. I do not know whether ten years of intoxication by hashish will bring about disasters equal to those caused by ten years of an opium diet; I do say that, at the actual time of consumption, and on the following day, hashish has more deadly results; the one is calm in its seduction, the other a demon in its dissolution.

In this latter part, I would like to describe and analyze the mental havoc caused by such delightfully dangerous capers – havoc so great, and danger so profound that anyone returning from battle no more than slightly scarred, reminds me of some stout soul who has escaped the cave of ever-changing Proteus, or of an Orpheus emerging victorious from Hell. Consider, if you will, that this form of language is excessively metaphorical; I will still maintain that the baneful stimulants strike me not only as one of the surest and most dreadful ways in which the Spirit of Darkness arranges to enlist and enslave wretched humanity, but even as one of the most perfect incorporations in his scheme.

This time, instead of assembling a collection of random anecdotes, I will attempt to shorten my task and make my analysis a bit clearer, by putting together a mass of observations centered about a single fictitious character. For this, I will need to imagine a person of my own choosing. In his *Confessions*, Dc Quincey rightly asserts that opium, instead of dulling a man, will stimulate him, but only along the natural lines of his personality; so that, if one were to judge of the marvels of opium, it would be absurd to refer to a cattle merchant; for such a one would dream only cows and pasture. Now, I am not about to describe the gross fantasies of a breeder stoned on opium; who would take pleasure in reading of *them?* Who would even *consent* to read them? If I am to conceptualize my subject, I must concentrate all its radii into a single circle, and polarize them; and the tragic circle into which I will assemble them will be, as I have said, a soul of my own choosing – something similar to what the eighteenth century called *l'homme sensible*, what the Romantic School termed *l'homme incompris*, and what the great houses and the bourgeoisie alike generally brand with the epithet of "unusual".

A temperament that mixes nervousness equally with passion would be most favorable to the evolution of such an intoxication; let us add a cultivated mind, trained by study of form and color; a tender heart, worn out by misery, but ever ready to be renewed; and, if you are willing, we will even go so far as to admit the existence of a few old failings, as well as what ought to result from them in any easily excitable nature – if not positive *remorse*, at least a regret for misspent and badly occupied time. A taste for metaphysics, and a knowledge of the various philosophical hypotheses about human destiny are certainly not useless complements – not any more so than is that love of Virtue, stoical or mystic Virtue, in the abstract, that has been supposed, in all the books on which our modern children feed, to be the highest pinnacle to which a well-bred individual can climb. If, to all that, we were to add a great refinement of the senses, which condition I omitted as being supererogatory, I believe that I would then have assembled all the most common universal elements of the modern *homme sensible*, the creature that could be called *the commonplace form of the unusual*. Let us now see what will become of such individuality when pushed to the utter limits by hashish. Let us follow along in this procession of man's conceit, up to its final and most resplendent altar, up to where the individual begins to believe in his own divinity.

If you are one of these souls, your innate love of form and color will initially find great pasturage in the earliest developments of your intoxication. Colors will assume unaccustomed strength, and will enter your mind with triumphant intensity. Ceiling frescoes – whether finely executed, mediocre, or even rather bad – will come alarmingly alive; the coarsest hangings plastering the walls of cheap hotels will deepen into splendid dioramas. Nymphs in radiant nudity will look down at you, their eyes deeper and clearer than water or sky; characters from antiquity, dressed out in all their priestly or military finery, will exchange solemn confidences with you through a simple look. The meandering of the lines is an absolutely clear language, in which you can read the restlessness and longing of their souls. Meanwhile, there is an evolvement of that mysterious and temporary mental state in which the whole extent of life, bristling with its many problems, is revealed in the scene (however natural and trivial it may be) before your eyes. Every thing that comes to your attention becomes a talking symbol. Fourier and Swedenborg, the one with his *analogies,* the other with his *correspondances*, have become incarnate in all things plant and animal that fall beneath your eyes; and instead of teaching verbally, they indoctrinate you through form and color. Your understanding of allegory assumes proportions unknown even to you; I will note, in passing, that the allegory, long an object of our scorn because of inept artists, but in reality a most *artful* form, one of the earliest and most natural forms of poetry, resumes its legitimate dominion in a mind enlightened by intoxication. The hashish spreads over all the world like a magic glaze; it solemnly tints it, and brings it light throughout. Craggy countrysides, receding horizons, city vistas whitened by the ghastly lividity of a storm, or lit by the dense heat of setting suns; spatial depth, which allegorizes temporal depth; the dancing and gestures and declamation of the players, if you have gone to the theatre; the first sentence that hits your eyes, if they should happen to fall upon a book; in short, everything – the whole universality of existence – rises before you with a new and hitherto unsuspected glory. Even grammar – sterile grammar, itself – becomes something like a sort of evocative witchcraft; words come to life, wrapped in flesh and bone – the noun, in all its substantive majesty; the adjective, transparent garb that dresses and colors it like glaze; and the verb, angel of motion, that sets the sentence moving. Music, that other language – dear to both the idle sorts and the profound natures that seek their diversion in the variety offered by work – speaks to you about *yourself*, and recites to you the poem of your life: it incorporates itself in you, and you melt into it. It speaks your passion – not in a vague, indefinite way, as it would at one of your casual evening affairs, or on an opera day, but in great detail, positively, each different tempo marking some familiar tempo of your soul, each note becoming transformed into a living word; and the entire poem enters your brain like a dictionary invested with a kind of life.

It should not be believed that all of these phenomena occur just helter-skelter in the mind, with all the discordant tone of reality, and all the disorder of the external world. The inner eye transforms all things, and presents each with whatever beauty it is lacking to be truly pleasure-inspiring. It is also to this essentially voluptuous and sensual stage that one must attribute the love for any clear water, whether running or still, that develops so astoundingly in the intoxicated brains of certain artists. Mirrors become a make-shift for such preoccupation, which resembles a sort of thirsting of the mind, and is conjoined with the throat-parching physical thirst I spoke of earlier; on-rushing water, sportive plays of water, melodious cascades, the blue immensity of the sea – all are there, rolling, singing, sleeping with an inexpressible charm. Water displays itself as a true enchantress; and although I do not much believe in the uncontrollable crazes said to be caused by hashish, I would not take it on oath that contemplation of a limpid pool was totally without danger for a mind enamored of space and crystal clarity; nor would I swear that the old story of the Water-sprite could not become a tragic reality for some enraptured soul.

I believe that I have spoken quite enough about the monstrous enlargement of time and space, two ideas that are always associated; now the mind is able to confront them without sadness or fear. With a certain melancholy delight, it gazes down, through the depths of ages, and boldly plunges into vistas infinite in scope. It has been understood, I presume, that this monstrous and tyrannical enlargement applies equally to all one's feeling and ideas: so it is with benevolence (I believe that I have presented a rather fine sample of this); so it is with one's notion of beauty; and so with love. The notion of beauty must naturally take possession of a vast area in the mental temperament that I have imagined. Harmony, balance of line, eurhythmy in all motion – to the dreamer these seem to be necessities, even *duties*, not only for all the beings of creation, but for him, himself – the dreamer who, at this period of the attack finds that he is endowed with a marvellous ability to understand the immortal and universal rhythm. And if our fanatic is wanting in personal beauty, do not think that he long suffers for having had to admit this, any more than that he regards himself as a discordant note in the world of harmony and beauty improvised by his imagination. The sophisms of hashish are many and admirable, generally tending toward optimism; and the most effective of these is the one that transforms desire into reality. Doubtless there are many similar situations in ordinary life, but how much more fervor and subtlety is to be found here! Besides, how could a creature so well equipped to understand harmony, a sort of priest of Beauty, possibly be an exception, a stain on his own theory? Intellectual beauty, with all its power; grace, with its seductions; eloquence, with its great prowess – all of these ideas soon present themselves, first as correctives for an indiscreet ugliness, then as consolers, and finally as the complete adulators of an imaginary sceptre.

As far as love is concerned, I have heard many people, moved by school-boy curiosity, seek to gain information from those who were familiar with the use of hashish. What could happen to the intoxication of love, already so powerful in its natural state, if it were embedded in the other intoxication, like a sun within a sun? Such is the question that springs up in a multitude of minds that I would like to refer to as the voyeurs of the mental world. To reply to a certain indecent innuendo – to that part of the question that doesn't dare come forth openly – I will refer the reader to Pliny, who somewhere or other spoke of the properties of hemp in such way as to dispel many illusions about the subject. Moreover, it is generally known that atony is the most usual resuit of man's abuse of his nerves and the substances designed to stimulate them. Now, as we are not now speaking of affective ability, but of feelings or sensitivities, I will simply beg the reader to consider that the imagination of a nervous man, intoxicated by hashish, is provoked to a stupendous degree, which can no more be determined than can the utmost possible force of the wind during a hurricane; and his senses have been sharpened to a point almost as difficult to define. So one may well imagine that a light touch, the most innocent conceivable – a handshake, for example – is capable of bearing one hundred times its ordinary weight because of the condition of the person's mind and senses; and such may even convey him, very rapidly, to that momentary lapse that vulgar mortals consider as the *summum bonum* of happiness. Now, there is no real question but that hashish, in a mind frequently concerned with love matters, awakens tender memories, which suffering and grief actually invest with a fresh new glow. And it is no less certain that a heavy dose of sensuality is mixed in with such stirrings of the soul; beyond this, it is not without use – and might well suffice to prove the immorality of hashish in this respect – to remark that a certain Ishmaelite sect (it is from the Ishmaelites that the Assassins are sprung) erringly switched its devotion from the impartial Lingam to the absolute and exclusive worship of the feminine version of the symbol. As each man is the living representation of history, it would be only natural to see a sort of obscene heresy, a monstrous religion, appear in a mind that has been shamefully abandoned to the mercy of an infernal drug – a mind that smiles at the destruction of its own abilities.

We have seen that during hashish intoxication there appears a most singular benevolence and goodwill, a kind of philanthropy, that extends even to strangers, and is made more of pity than of love (it is in this that we find the embryo of the satanic spirit that will soon develop in an extraordinary manner) – a benevolence that goes even to the point of fear of hurting anyone at all; from this we may guess at what could happen to a localized sentimentality, applied to some dearly loved person who plays or has played an important role in the mental life of the experimenter. Worship, adoration, prayer, and dreams of happiness surge up and are projected with the ambitious energy and sudden flare of fireworks; like the explosive powders and coloring chemicals of a pyrotechnic display, they blaze up and vanish in the darkness. There is no kind of sentimental combination to which the pliant love of a hashish slave cannot lend itself. A desire to protect, a feeling of sincere paternal devotion, may be mixed with a sinful sensuality that the hashish is always able to excuse and absolve. It goes even further. Let us suppose that certain mistakes have been made, and that these have left their bitter marks upon the soul, so his stormy past with sadness; in hashish, this bitterness may turn that husband or lover, in his normal state, will only contemplate sweet; the need for forgiveness makes one's imagination at once more adept and more desperately beseeching; and in this diabolical drama that is expressed only by a lengthy monologue, remorse itself may act as a stimulant, and serve powerfully to rekindle the heart's old passion. Yes, remorse! Was I wrong to say that to a truly philosophical soul hashish must seem a perfectly satanic instrument? Remorse, that most singular ingredient of pleasure, soon is drowned in the delicious *contemplation* of remorse, in a kind of voluptuous analysis; and this analysis is so rapid that man, that natural devil (to speak in Swedenborgian terms), does not perceive how involuntary it is, or how, from second to second, he is drawing nearer to a diabolical perfection. He *admires* his remorse, and glorifies himself, while he is in the very process of losing his liberty.

So there you have my imaginary man, the soul of my own choosing, finally arrived at such a degree of joy and serenity that he is *forced* to admire himself. All contradiction is wiped out, all philosophical problems become crystal-clear, or at least appear so. Everything is cause for further joy. The fullness of his present life excites enormous joy within him. A voice speaks inside him (alas! it is his own) and says, "Now you have the right to consider yourself superior to all men; no one either knows or is capable of understanding all the things that you think and feel; people would even be incapable of appreciating the kindness that they inspire in you. You are a *king* who has been left unnoticed by the commoners along the way, a king who is alone in his conviction that he is one: but what matters t to you? Do you not possess that sovereign scorn that so uplifts the soul?"

Still, we might suppose that from time to time some stinging memory or other could cut through this happiness, corrupting it. Some suggestion furnished by the outside world might come to revive a past that is disagreeable to contemplate. How filled with vile or foolish actions is the past-actions that are truly unworthy of such a king of the mind, and blemish his ideal dignity. Understand that a man on hashish will confront such reproachful phantoms bravely, and will even be able to derive new elements of pleasure and pride from these hideous memories. His reasoning will evolve in this manner: when the first feeling of grief has passed, he will carefully analyze the action or emotion whose memory it was that disturbed the present moment of his glory; he will consider the motives that had made him act, and the circumstances in which he had found himself at the time; and if he does not find these circumstances sufficient, if not to excuse his sin, then at very least to lighten it, do not imagine for a moment that he feels defeated! I can look in upon his reasoning just as I can watch the functioning of some mechanism beneath a transparent pane of glass: "This ridiculous (or vile) (or cowardly) action, which was just now painful for me to remember, is completely out of keeping with my true nature, my present nature; and the very zeal with which I am condemning it, the inquisitorial care with which I am analyzing and judging it, serve to prove my lofty and divine capacity for virtue. How many are there in the world of men as able as I to judge themselves, or as severe in self-condemnation?" And not only does he condemn himself, but exalts himself as well. Once the dreadful memory has thus been absorbed in contemplation of an ideal virtue, an ideal generosity, an ideal talent, he is ready to yield openly to his triumphant spiritual debauch. We have seen how, in a sacrilegious counterfeit of the sacrament of penitence, our man – at once both penitent and confessor – granted himself an easy absolution, or, worse yet, derived from his self-condemnation still more fodder for his pride. Now, contemplation of his dreams and plans of virtue lead him to infer his practical ability to be virtuous; the loving energy with which he embraces this virtue-fantasy seems to him to be proof enough of the *virile* energy necessary to accomplish his idea. He completely confuses the dream with the action; and as his imagination has waxed warmer and warmer before the beguiling spectacle of his own nature at its correctest and most ideal, gradually substituting this fascinating image of himself for the *real* individual, poor in will and rich in vanity, he ends by decreeing his apotheosis in the following clear and simple terms, which contain a whole world of abominable pleasures for him: "I am the most virtuous of men!"

Does that not remind you of Jean-Jacques Rousseau, who also, after confessing to all the universe (and not without a certain pleasure), dared to raise the self-same cry of triumph (or at least, any difference was very slight) with the very same sincerity and conviction? The zeal with which he admired virtue, the keen compassion that filled his eyes with tears at the very sight of any noble action, or even the thought of some noble action that he would like to perform, were quite enough to give him a very superlative idea of his moral worth. Jean-Jacques had become intoxicated *without* hashish.

Shall I carry the analysis of this triumphant monomania even farther? Shall I explain how, under the influence of the poison, our man soon makes himself the centre of the universe? Or how he becomes the ultimate living expression of the proverb that claims that passion fetches all things to herself? He believes in his virtue and talent; can the reader not guess the end? All of the objects about him are just so many suggestions to stir up a world of thoughts within him, all more highly-colored, more alive, more subtle than ever, and covered over by a magic glaze. "These magnificent cities," says he to himself, "with their superb buildings arranged row on row, as if in some theatrical set; – these lovely ships, just rocking gently on the open sea, in nostalgic idleness, and seeming to express our thought: When will we be on our way for Happiness? – these museums, simply flowing over with beautiful forms and intoxicating colors; – these libraries, where the studies of Science and the dreamings of the Muse have been collected; – these musical instruments that have been put together so that all will speak with but a single voice; – these captivating women, all the more charming for their skill in dressing and their modesty of look; – all these things were created *for me, for me, for me!* For me, humanity has toiled, and has been sacrificed and martyred – to serve as pasturage or pabulum for my implacable hungering for knowledge, beauty, and emotion!" I am skipping and abridging. It will amaze no one that one last, supreme thought comes bursting from the dreamer's brain: "I have become God!" This wild and savage cry bounds from his chest with such force, such power of projection, that, if the strength of will and the sincere beliefs of a man grown drunk had any efficacy whatever, it would cause the downfall of the angels from the skies: "I am a God!" But by and by, this tempest of pride is transformed into the fairer weather of a silent, calm, refreshed beatitude; and all the universality of creation appears as if lit and colored by a sulfurous dawn. And if, by chance, some vague remembrance should happen to slip into the mind of this beatific wretch, – "Might there not be another God?" – you may be sure that he will stand up straight even before Him, and discuss his whims, and face Him without fear. Who was the French philosopher who sought to make jest of the modern Germans by saying, "Am I, then, a god who has dined poorly?" Such sarcasm would not seem cutting to a mind grown high on hashish; it would answer, tranquilly, "It is possible that I have dined poorly, but I am a God."

V

Moral

Ah, but the Morning After! That terrible Morning After! Your drained, exhausted body, your unstrung nerves, a certain titillating desire to cry, and the fact that it is impossible for you to apply yourself to any sustained work-all are cruelly teaching you that you have played at a forbidden game. Hideous nature, stripped of the illumination of the night before, now resembles the cheerless trash left over from a party. It is especially your will -most precious of all your faculties-that has been attacked. They say, (and it is *almost* true,) that the substance causes no physical harm, or at least no *serious* harm. But even if a man's body were in good condition, could it really be asserted that he was truly *well,* if he were incapable of any positive action, and fit only to dream? Now, we understand human nature quite well enough to know that a man who can instantly procure all wealth in heaven and earth with a single teaspoonful of jelly, will never earn the slightest fraction of it by working. Can anyone imagine a State whose citizens all were in the habit of becoming intoxicated on hashish? Fine citizens, *they!* fine warriors! fine legislators! Even in the Orient, where its use is so widespread, there are governments that have understood the necessity of banning it.

Indeed, man is forbidden, under pain of decadence and intellectual death, to disturb the primordial conditions of his existence, or to break the balance between his mind and the environment in which it is destined to function; in a word, he is forbidden to disturb his destiny for the sake of supplanting it with a new kind of fate. Let us recall that admirable symbol, Melmoth. His dreadful suffering lay in the disproportion between the wonderful abilities he had instantly acquired through a satanic pact, and the surroundings in which, as a creature of God, he was condemned to live. And no one he attempted to entice would consent to buy his terrible prerogative from him on the same terms. Any man who doesn't accept the terms of life, does, in effect, sell his soul. It is easy to grasp the connection that exists between the satanic creations of the poets and the real-life creatures that have consecrated themselves to stimulants. Man has wanted to be God; and by and by, here he is, by virtue of some unverifiable moral law, fallen even lower than usual. His soul is being sold piecemeal.

Balzac doubtless believed that there was no greater shame, no keener suffering for man than the renunciation of his will. I saw him, once, at a gathering where they were discussing the wonderful effects of hashish. He was listening and asking questions with an amusingly lively attention. People who knew him understood that he must be interested. But the idea of having to think *in spite of himself* was extremely offensive to him. Someone handed him some dawamesk; he examined it, sniffed it, and returned it – untouched. The struggle between his almost child-like curiosity and his reluctance to yield revealed itself strikingly in his expressive face. He was carried away by his passion for self-respect. It is indeed difficult to imagine the theorist of the *Will*, Louis Lambert's spiritual double, consenting to be deprived of that precious "substance".

Despite the admirable service that ether and chloroform have rendered, it seems to me that, from the point of view of spiritualist philosophy, the same moral blemish applies to all modern inventions that tend to diminish human liberty and eliminate indispensable pain. It was not without a kind of admiration that I once heard the paradox of a certain officer, who told me of the painful operation performed upon a French general at El-Aghouat – an operation from which the latter died, the chloroform notwithstanding. This general was a very brave man; and even more, he was one of those souls to whom the term "chivalrous" applies quite naturally. "It wasn't chloroform he needed," the officer told me, "but the attention of the whole army, and the regimental music. Maybe that way he would have recovered!" The surgeon wasn't of a mind with this officer; but undoubtedly the chaplain would have admired his sentiments.

After all of these considerations, it is really superfluous to keep stressing the immoral character of hashish. If I were to compare it to suicide – a slow suicide – an ever-bloodied, ever-sharpened weapon, no reasonable mind would fault me for it. If I were to liken it to sorcery and witchcraft (which operate upon matter, using secret rites whose efficacy can in no way be either proven or disproven, in an attempt to gain an ascendancy forbidden to man, or permitted only to men deemed worthy of it) no philosophical soul would condemn such comparison. If the Church condemns witchcraft and sorcery, it is because they militate against the intentions of God, eliminate the workings of Time, and seek to render purity and morality superfluous; and the Church considers as true and legitimate only such wealth as has been earned through assiduous good works. The gambler who has found a sure "system", we brand as a "shark"; what name will we give to the man who tries to buy happiness and talent with a few coins? It is the very infallibility of the method that constitutes its immorality, just as the supposed infallibility of witchcraft imposes an infernal stigma upon *it*. Need I add that hashish, like all solitary pleasures, makes the individual useless to his fellow men, and renders society superfluous for the individual? It leads a man to admire himself endlessly, day by day precipitating him nearer the brink of the luminous gulf where he beholds in admiration his Narcissus-face.

And yet, what if – even at the price of his dignity, integrity and free will – man could derive some great intellectual benefit from hashish, making it a sort of thinking-machine, a productive implement? This is a question that I have often heard asked, and I will answer it. First of all, as I have explained at length, hashish reveals nothing to the individual but the individual, himself. It is true that he has been raised to the third power, as it were, and has grown extraordinarily; and as it is equally certain that memory of one's impressions will live on after the debauch, it would seem, at first appearance, that the anticipations of the "utilitarians" in this respect are not entirely stripped of reason. But I would beg them to take note that the thoughts they are counting on to yield such great advantage are not really as beautiful as they appear beneath their temporary disguise, draped in magic tinsel. They are of the earth, rather than of heaven; and they owe a large part of their beauty to nervous excitement, and to the eagerness with which the mind pounces upon them. This anticipation, then, is a vicious circle. Let us admit, for the moment, that hashish yields talent, or at least *increases* it; they are still forgetting that it is in the nature of hashish to diminish the Will, so that with one hand it imparts what it snatches back with the other. In other words, it yields imagination, without the ability to profit by it. Finally, even supposing that there were a man clever and spirited enough to escape this alternative, we must still bear in mind another dread, inevitable danger, which accompanies all *habits*. Soon enough, they all turn into *needs*. A person who resorts to poison *to help him* think, by and by will no longer be able to *think without its help*. Can you imagine the horrible lot of a man whose crippled imagination could no longer function without the aid of hashish or opium?

In philosophical studies, the human mind mirrors the revolution of the spheres, and is obliged to follow a curve that will return it to the point of its departure. To conclude is only to complete a circle. I began by speaking of that wondrous state in which the mind of man occasionally finds itself, as if through favor of a special grace; I said that man's endless longing to rekindle his hopes and rise to infinity, has led him, in every age and clime, to display a frantic craving for any substance – dangerous or not – that could excite his individuality, and set before his eyes, if only for an instant, the second-hand paradise that was the object of his every desire; and it is in this way that man's daring soul – *en route* to hell without quite knowing it – has given proof of its original greatness. But man is not so forsaken, so deprived of any *honest* means of reaching heaven, that he should be obliged to turn to pharmacy and witchcraft; he need not sell his soul to pay for the intoxicating kisses and affection of the Houri. A fine Paradise it is that is bought at the price of one's eternal salvation! I am picturing a man (shall I make him a Brahman, a poet or a Christian philosopher?) stationed atop the lofty summit of the Olympus that is Spirituality; all about him, the Muses of Raphael or Mantegna compose their sublimest dances to solace him for his long fastings and constant prayers; and they gaze upon him softly, with their brightest smiles; divine Apollo, master of every art (Francavilla's, Dürer's, Goltzius', or any other man's – what does it matter? Does not Apollo exist for every man that is worthy of him?), gently sets his bow to the most vibrant strings. Below him, in the muck and brambles at the foot of the mountain, the throng of humans – sad little company of helots – counterfeits a grin of pleasure, and shrieks at the sting of the poison; and the poet, saddened, reflects: "Poor souls, who have neither fasted nor prayed, and have refused to be redeemed through work! Now they seek in black magic a way of rising, one-two-three, to a more-than-natural level of existence. The magic cheats them, and kindles for them the false flame of false happiness; whereas we, the poets and philosophers, have regenerated our souls through constant work and meditation; through the conscientious use of our Will, and the enduring loftiness of our Purpose, we have made ourselves a garden of true beauty. Trusting in the promise that faith can move mountains, we have performed the only miracle permitted us by God."